*Everybody Is Special*

# *Everybody Is Special*

by

Gary E. Mann

· Mercer University Press ·

ISBN 0-86554-451-4 MUP/H358

*Everybody Is Special*

Mercer University Press, Macon, Georgia 31207

Printed in the United States of America

❑

The paper used in this publication meets the minimum requirements of American National Standard for Information Sciences—Permanence of Paper for Printed Library Materials, ANSI Z39.48–1984.

❑

*Library of Congress Cataloging-in-Publication Data*
Gary E. Mann, 1958– .
Everybody is special / by Gary E. Mann.
xviii+166 pp. 6x9" (15x23cm.).
ISBN 0-86554-451-4
1. Mann, Gary E., 1958– .
2. Cerebral palsied—United States—Biography.
I. Title.
RC388.M264 1994
362.1'968360092—dc20
[B] 94-31282
CIP

# *Contents*

# *List of Illustrations (A Photo album)*

# *A Foreword*

*by Ferrol Sams*

Prolapse of the cord! These are words that produce frenetic activity on any obstetrical floor. That silvery slippery lifeline, the conduit of all nutrients from mother to unborn child, must at all costs remain intact until the baby is born. During labor the muscular sphere that for nine months has been a placid, nurturing nest that accepted a polliwog and succored it from embryo to fetus to manchild is transformed. It becomes, under the burgeoning moon, a raging dreadnought that squeezes with such rhythmic and crushing force that its parasitic passenger is propelled, shivering and howling, into an alien world.

During this process called labor, rarely and without warning, the umbilical cord can slither prematurely to the outside and be so compressed during uterine contractions that the blood flow carrying oxygen to the newborn brain is impaired.

When this happens, the nurses and doctors have a minimum of time in which to avert catastrophe. Rapid caesarean section is imperative. Without oxygen this baby will die. Or, more challengingly, this baby may live. At such a moment, quality of life becomes a paramount issue. Everyone is conscious of the sure and mysterious hand of God, and mortal man, working frantically, prays fervently. Sometimes one is confused about how he should phrase his prayer.

Oxygen deprivation to the brain is comparable to loss of electric current from a fuse box. Any or all of the circuits may be affected. The lights may go out permanently in the sacred chamber where intelligence is housed. Vision may be completely destroyed. The channels that control muscular activity may also be so underserved that one shambles instead of walking. Slowly writhing, snake-like motions can alternate with uncontrollable jerking until even speech becomes a travesty.

This is a most horrible garden of the witches. It is called cerebral palsy.

Like all medical conditions, this one affects individuals with varying degrees of intensity. It can kill rapidly. The limp and limber newborn may never breathe, may never move, may shade under the delivery room lamps from dusky blue to the terrible whiteness that defies recall to life. Joy, hope, and expectation shrivel in the mother's breast to be carried ever thereafter as a scar, silent, unsung, but constantly present, as white and unresponsive as her dead baby.

On the other hand, the mills of the gods can grind slow but exceeding fine, and cerebral palsy can kill very gradually. Witness a thrity-five-year-old caricature of a man, almost a mummy. He is sightless, mindless, mute. He lies curled like a fetus and does not move his limbs. His snags of useless teeth are almost buried in fungoid mounds of overly reddened gums that have resulted from his medication. By the calendar and clock this is a man, but he weighs no more than fifty pounds.

He is dependent for water, food, and diapers upon a constantly attending slave who is called his mother. The room in which he exists is kept very quiet, is darkened to forestall rending seizures. It is a somber room, the air dry and leached of joy. The Cross is serious business and it is present in this room. There was gambling but no laughter at Calvary. Cerebral palsy is an insult to godhead.

This book that Gary Mann has written is a travelogue. It is the itinerary of a life. It recounts the journey of a family through the land of cerebral palsy in company with a man whose oxygen supply was interrupted during birth, but under conditions that while crippling him physically, spared his sparkling intelligence.

The author himself is a victim, but he refuses to see himself as such. He is, instead, a conqueror, looking always forward and upward, defiantly spurning the mud wallow of self-pity.

He tells his story in simple prose—terse, objective, factual, a style required of journalists in yesteryears before permissible editors allowed simpering editorializing to be presented as news stories. He gives out the facts. He leaves room for the reader's imagination to roam.

One can envision the shock, the anguish, the despair, even the ensuing rage of upper-middle-class parents confronted with this unexpected natal gift, but it is not delineated.

One can trace in this account the development of dogged determination in the father, sense the daily drudgery of the trapped mother, speculate on the embarrassment of siblings at this different child in their midst, guess at the bewildered hurt of the rejected adolescent, but the reader must do all this for himself. The author does not line it out for him.

This is a book filled with cheerfulness, with joy. Caring and helpful people troop through its pages and are recognized. It is a tribute to family support, to church and community support, and to institutional support by a dedicated university for one lone individual. That individual, Gary Mann, manifests anew the Greek axiom: Mind is mistress of man. It also demonstrates Jesus' promise that the yoke is easy and the burden light.

Gary Mann has approached the hurdles of his life with determination, but also with zest. In the end he has prevailed. The cross is present in his journey as well as in the darkened room, but when borne on the shoulders of many there is happiness and laughter. The Cross, after all, was also the Throne of Christ.

Gary Mann, triumphant once more, deserves yet another standing ovation for his work.

*—Ferrol Sams*

# *A Foreword*

## *by John R. Irwin IV*

I met Gary Mann when I was assigned to Riverside United Methodist Church in Macon, Georgia, as the associate pastor with responsibility for the youth program. One of my counselors approached me with the message that Gary wanted to work with the youth. Could he do it? Gary takes longer to walk somewhere, to eat a meal, to get out a sentence than most people. Sometimes it is extremely difficult to understand him. *Could* he do it? *Would* the youth respond to him? Would he try it for a while—for every Sunday evening, special activities, overnight trips out of town—and then quit?

For five years, as I worked with the youth, the staff, and the other counselors, Gary was there. Could he do it? Yes he could! The youth continue to respond to him very well. He carries his share of responsibility on Sunday evenings, he is very regular, has presented the program several times, participates in special activities, and goes with us on trips. For example, when we snow ski, Gary can't, so he keeps up with the youth who don't ski.

Gary loves the church, and especially loves the youth. He is filled with joy, and usually there's a big smile on his face.

When someone asks me if he is handicapped, I have to think for a moment before I respond, "I guess so."

To be honest, there are some things Gary can't do. He can't sell over the phone, he won't win a race running, he can't drive alone, and he won't break a record for typing a large number of words per minute.

Yet I would describe my friend as someone with a big heart, a giant soul, and a great mind trapped in a body that doesn't quite work as it was designed to work. I know other people who are "handicapped" with all their physical properties in order, yet who are lacking in spirit, compassion, caring, and kindness. Those are the ones I feel sorry for, but not for Gary Mann.

*—John R. Irwin IV*

# *A Preface*

*by David S. Mann*

This is Gary's story. Though born with cerebral palsy, he has overcome one obstacle after another to lead an almost normal life. And he has done this with such good humor that he has captivated most everyone who has come into contact with him. I believe his optimistic outlook comes through in this narrative.

Against many expert judgments he has learned to write in script, to type, to walk unaided, to drive a car, to sing in a choir, to go camping, to transfer from special to regular education and to graduate from high school and college, to do computer data entry, to be gainfully employed, and to do many other things.

His mother and I, the rest of the family, and his many friends are proud of him. His self-image is great. He never had to be begged to study. His drive to improve has always been tremendous.

In his mid-teens he conceived of writing this book, essentially his autobiography. He has been working on it off and on ever since.

I hope this book will be of interest to a general audience, and that it will be of help and possible inspiration to other handicapped people and their families. I also hope the reader will get a better insight into and understanding of the handicapped. In actual life I feel Gary's teachers and other mentors often learned as much from him as he did from them. I know I have, and continue to do so.

*—David S. Mann, Gary Mann's father*

# *Acknowledgments*

I am thankful for so many people and forces helping me through life and in writing this book, that it is difficult to know where to start in acknowledging them.

First of all, my life has been blessed by a good Lord. Without Him none of my accomplishments would have been possible. A lot of things experts told my parents I would never be able to do I have done, such as go to regular school, walk unassisted, learn to type, and lead a near-normal life.

My family has always been most supportive, and they have my everlasting thanks. My father has fought for my right to get an education, and for my right to enjoy all life's benefits as unhandicapped persons do.

My mother has been of great importance in my life. My father was gone all day and even part of the night with his busy medical practice, but my mother was *always* there, helping me all day and constantly chauffering me to schools and various therapies.

My older brother David has always looked out for me. He has spent innumerable hours and much effort editing this book, to be repaid only with love and gratitude.

My sister Beverly has been the most loving sister anyone could have. When I was small she was my "Second Momma" and always comforted me.

Clark, the brother next to me, wrestled with me, taught me to be "one of the boys," and all about snakes and animals.

Everyone in my family helped teach me to walk, by walking me around the room while holding my hands over my head.

Uncle Joe and Aunt Mary Helen Daniel have given me loving attention and have come to my rescue many times. So did my Aunt Elizabeth and Uncle Tag Denton before they died. My Aunt Lil and

Uncle Jack Watt have always encouraged me. Uncle Harold and Aunt Betty Mann have been interested in my progress.

My four grandparents lived in Macon and were always wonderful to me. (I am sorry they are dead.) I have written about my daddy's father, Rev. David G. Mann, in this book (especially chapter 12). His wife Gertrude was an invalid for many years before her death, but she loved me, and I loved her.

"MaMa Daniel," my other grandmother, loved me as much as anyone could, as did my other grandfather "PaPa Daniel."

My cousin Bonny Gibson and her husband Billy, who live in Macon, have stood by me many times.

Jane McKissack and dozens of other cousins have given me love and encouragement. Deryl Hoyal has helped me especially, with jobs and in other ways.

Many healthcare professionals, therapists, doctors, and other specialized people have worked with me and helped me. There is no way to mention all of them, but I thank each and every one. The late William Burgamy, a registered physical therapist, worked diligently with me for more than ten years, and he was more responsible for my being able to walk and have good muscle strength than any other one individual. The best physical therapist I had after him was Mrs. Margaret Podlesny. Mrs. Theo Fisher, an occupational therapist, taught me to type, for which I am eternally grateful, and she remains a great friend to this day. Dr. Richard Logan, a speech therapist, and Mrs. Filomena Mullis, my reading instructor, helped me for many years. I am grateful to Dr. Marshall Allen, who did the brain pacemaker surgery on me.

In elementary special education, I am particularly indebted to the late Mrs. Dorothy Poythress, Mrs. Carolyn Riley, and Mrs. Exie Williams.

At the Tinsley Special Education school Janie, the maid, helped me a lot. She was later replaced by Louvenia ("Lou") Tolliver, who was great too. The late C. J. James, the janitor, was my buddy. I enjoyed kidding with all of them.

In my transfer from special to regular education I especially thank Ms. Ann Henry, the curriculum coordinator. More than anyone else, she helped me to become the first multihandicapped student to be fully mainstreamed in the Bibb County public school system.

I am grateful to then-Superintendent Dr. Thomas Lott. I also thank Dr. Richard Ludlam, Mrs. Bettye Parker, and Elton Wall. Many others in the Bibb County schools also supported me.

At Mercer University I greatly appreciate the efforts of Mary Jane Pollitzer (now Stewart), my counselor. Dr. Thomas Glennon, my main advisor, straightened out my major, and remains a good friend. My Kappa Alpha fraternity brothers literally helped "carry" me through Mercer. Many other people at Mercer also aided me.

A great friend and constant booster is Mrs. Patsy Fried, who has done uncountable good deeds for me, and who has been a friend of my mother's since their teens. Another special person is Dr. Barbara Clinton, who worked with me many hours on the computer, has given and found me jobs, and who is a true friend.

I thank the people who make up the chapters in this book, and all the ministers and assistants who have been at Riverside United Methodist Church, especially Rev. John Irwin.

Others I thank are Flynn and Gina Partain, and those in my Sunday School classes. I give a special tribute to my very good friend Tracy Jones (now Johns), who has pulled me through many a rough time.

I want to thank my professional author friend Albert Kirby Griffin, who has assisted me immensely with the technicalities of writing.

I continue to have some close and loyal college and fraternity friends, especially Hank Clay, Johnny Davis, Jon Dean, Chuck Lanford, and Dave Rozier.

I also greatly thank my computer expert friend Fred Dismuke for much help, especially for putting the entire manuscript on diskettes in ASCII for the publisher.

In addition, Robert Hall, Dell Bunker, Bobby and Tee George, George Patterson, Pat and Donna Patterson, Phil and Sharon McRae, John Mitchell, Jr., Tom Hall, Earl and Adela Ford, Tommy and Paula Wyatt, Jeff and Jennifer Everett, and others have been very good to me. I thank these and the many others who have helped me.

I love you all.

*—Gary Mann*

❑

*To my late grandfather*
*Rev. David G. Mann,*

*and to my parents*
*Dr. David S. Mann and Joyce Mann*

❑

# *Everybody Is Special: A Photo Album*

Everybody *is* special. In this album are a few special scenes from my life, and photos of some of the special people in my life. I wish I had pictures or room on these pages to show more.

*1. At my college graduation, I seem to be contemplating my future and remembering the special people in my life.*

*2. Macon Hospital, Macon, Georgia, where I was born.*

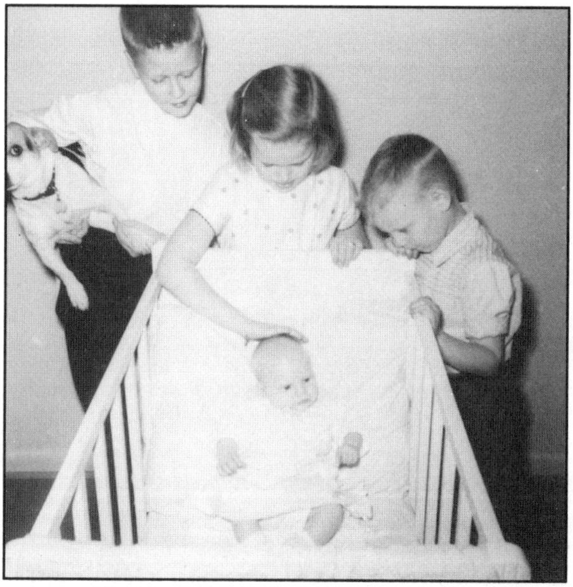

3. *My sister Beverly pats my head as my brothers David and Clark look on.*

*4. A Christmas card photo of me as an infant, with David, Clark, and Beverly.*

*5. Neighborhood children visit. (Beverly is holding me, at left.)*

*6. At about 18 months of age, I could not walk, but I could get around very well in this stroller.*

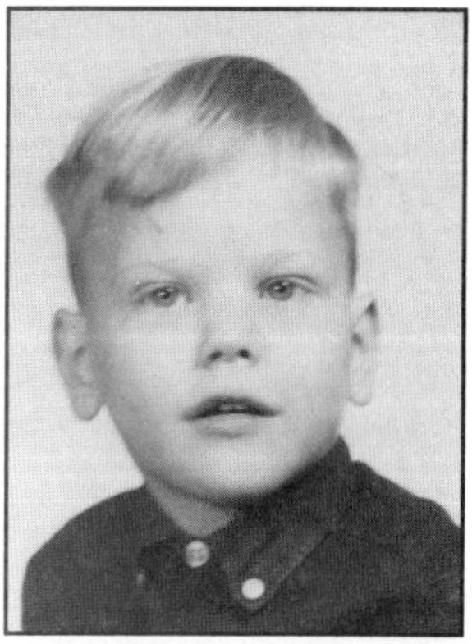

*7. This was my school picture, at age 5.*

*8. Here I am holding Caesar and Beau (about mid-January 1971).*

*9. When this family portrait was taken I was 7 years old.*

*10. Playing with Schatzie and Chico, MaMa Daniel's dog, in our front yard.*

*11. My mother and father, Dr. David S. and Joyce Mann, dressed for a party.*

*12. PaPa and MaMa (Joseph W., Sr., and Bonnylin) Daniel.*

*13. PaPa and MaMa Mann (Rev. David G. and Gertrude Mann) at their golden wedding anniversary, Riverside United Methodist Church.*

*14. PaPa Mann and his new bride Clariece, just married by Rev. Reece Turrentine, our minister, during the morning church service.*

*15. Aunt Elizabeth and Uncle Tag (Fred Lester Denton) with their children Bonny and Deryl and their families.*

*16. Uncle Harold (Dr. Harold H. Mann) and Aunt Betty with their children Janet, Martha, and Hal.*

*17. Uncle Joe and Aunt Mary Helen (Dr. and Mrs. Joe W. Daniel) with their children Joey, Debby, Bennett, Freddy, and Bonnylin.*

*18. Aunt Lil and Uncle Jack (Dr. and Mrs. John R. Watt) and their children Cathy, David, and Madeleine.*

*19. Cousins Jane and Herb McKissack with their daughter Kim.*

20. *Nephew Daniel Chance is engrossed in the book "Uncle Gary" is reading to him.*

*21. Our 1993 family portrait. Left to right, front row: me (Gary), Tina, Christy (daughter of Clark and Tina), Mother, my sister Beverly, and Beverly's son Daniel; back row: my brother Clark, Daddy, and my brother David.*

*22. Entrance to T. D. Tinsley School of Special Education, which I attended for many years.*

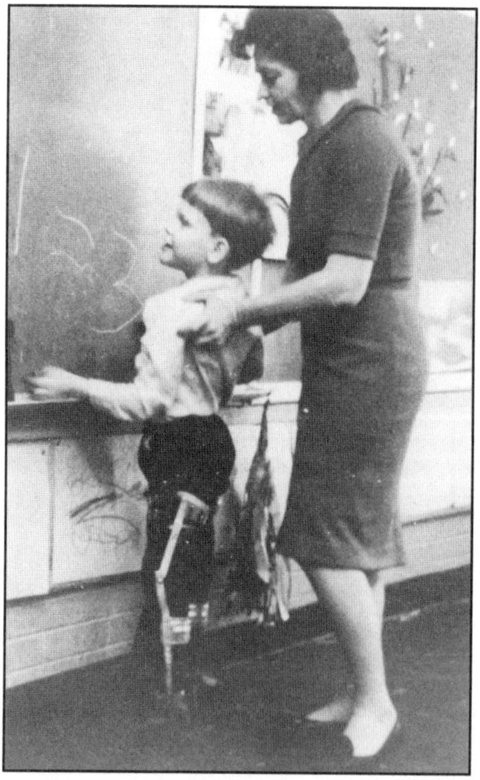

*23. Mrs. Caroline Riley, my first special education teacher. I started with her when I was 4 years old.*

*24. I am standing and working at the chalkboard in Mrs. Riley's beginning special education class.*

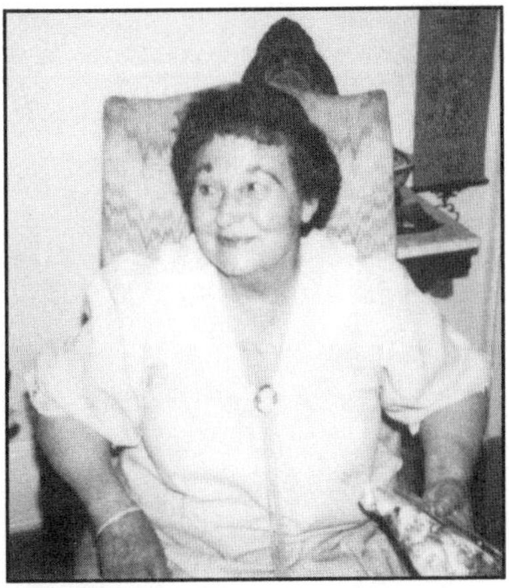

*25. Mrs. Exie Williams, my upper special education teacher at Tinsley.*

*26. Mrs. Hudson, my math teacher at T. D. Tinsley School. I was allowed to attend her class for 45 minutes daily in regular school. This was my first step toward being "mainstreamed" from special education into regular school.*

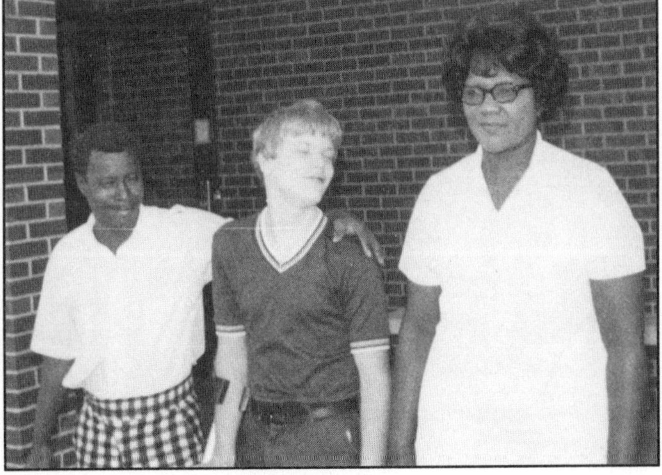

*27. Bobby and Lou, helpers at the Tinsley School of Special Education.*

*28. Horse rides and hamburgers, big treats for the students and staff of Tinsley Special Education. Annually Patsy Fried and family have a picnic and entertain. I am in the middle with a cane and patting the horse.*

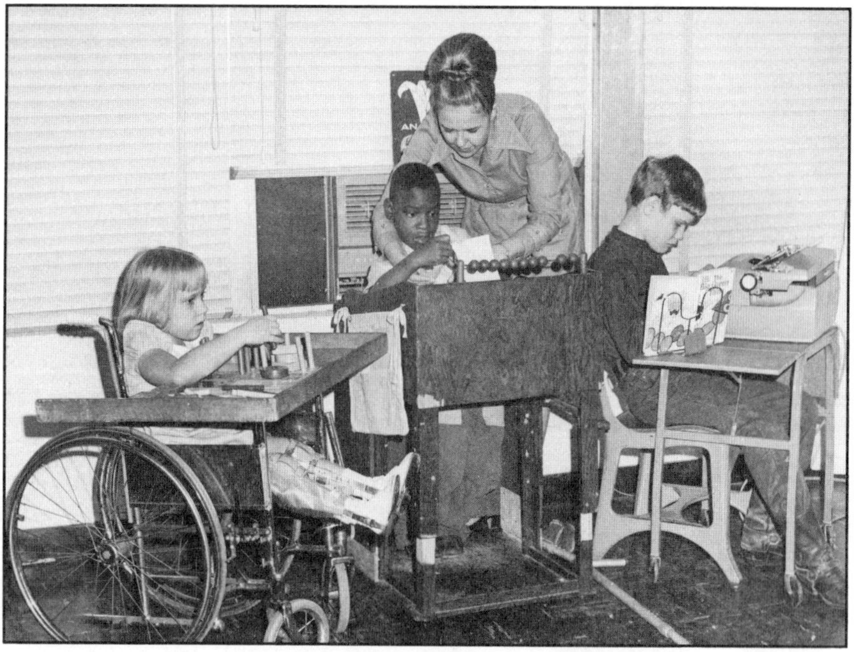

*29. When I was 10, the Easter Seal occupational therapist, Mrs. Theo Fisher, pictured here in a typical classroom scene, started teaching me to type.*

*30. Part of the approximately 3,500-pupil Ballard Hudson complex in Macon, the first public high school I was transferred to from sheltered special education. This is part of Ballard B Junior High School, where I entered the eighth grade; I also went here for the ninth grade.*

*31. In the halls of Ballard B. (This photo was taken by Mrs. Gardner, my ninth grade English teacher.)*

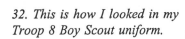

*32. This is how I looked in my Troop 8 Boy Scout uniform.*

*33. Central (Lanier) Senior High School. I attended Central for grades 10 through 12, and graduated. Central's nickname is "The Big Orange."*

*34. With me here is one of my Central professors, Wardlow Johnson, whom I nicknamed "Peanut."*

*35. Bettye Parker, my history teacher at Lanier, and I take a stroll when we met her on our New England trip.*

*36. This is Jennie, my high school friend whom I wrote about.*

*37. My occupational therapist Theo Fisher and former teachers Mrs. Riley and Mrs. Williams all came to my high school graduation.*

*38. This was my formal high school graduation picture (1979).*

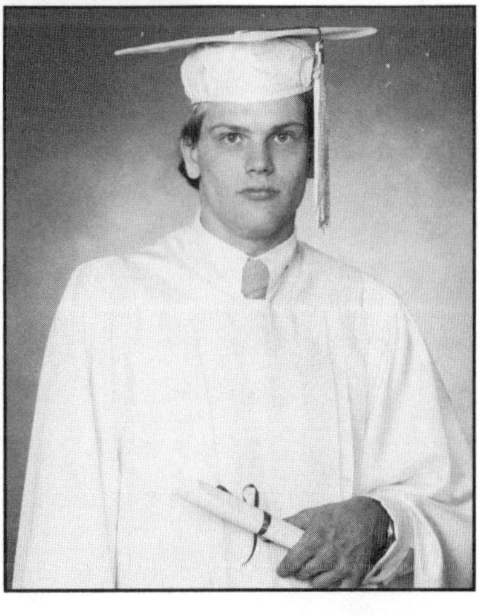

*39. Riverside United Methodist Church in Macon. I have been active here all my life, joining at age 13. The youth group and choirs have meant much to me, and I have now been a youth counselor for many years.*

*40. Riverside United Methodist youth and the van in a group picture at the beginning of one of our many church tours.*

*41. PaPa Mann (Rev. David G. Mann) in the pulpit at Riverside Methodist Church.*

*42. PaPa Mann hands me the first shovelful of dirt for the groundbreaking for the new sanctuary. I was on my way home from the hospital. This was in 1976.*

*43. Rev. John Irwin IV, associate pastor of Riverside United Methodist Church, who wrote an introduction to my book.*

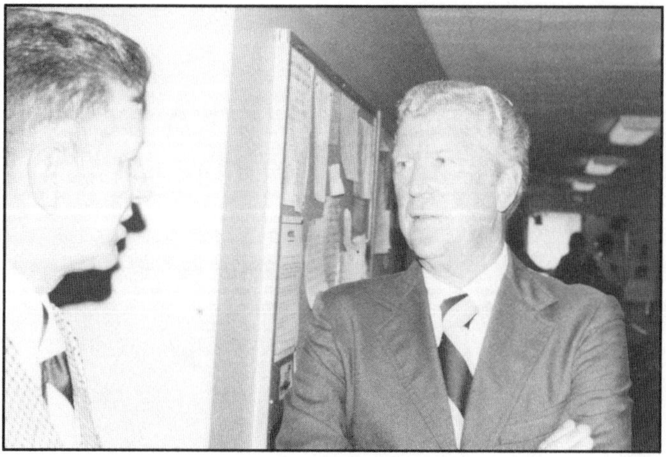

*44. World-famous New York neurosurgeon the late Dr. Irving A. Cooper, who devised the "brain pacemaker" surgery. To the left is my Macon neurosurgeon and friend Dr. Hugh Smisson.*

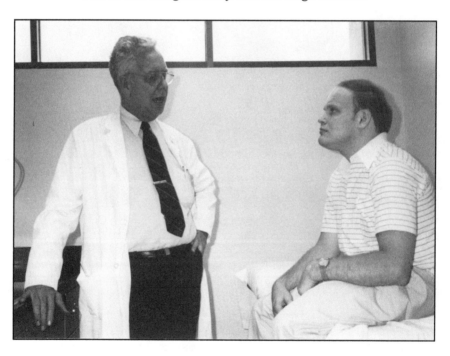

*45. Dr. Marshall B. Allen, Jr., Chief of Neurosurgery at the Medical College of Georgia in Augusta discusses the "brain pacemaker" operation with me. He did that surgery.*

*46. The towers of Mercer University, Macon, Georgia.*

*47. Tom Glennon, my Mercer professor and advisor, who greatly helped me straighten out my major.*

*48. Tracy Jones (now Johns)—always a great pal, who encouraged me when I was depressed.*

*49. My first KA "little brother," Mark Brittain.*

*50. For my sophomore KA Old South Ball, I am dressed in a Confederate uniform and my date Belinda wears a hoop skirt.*

*51. Here I am dancing with my date Lee Strickland at my last KA Old South Ball at Mercer.*

*52. Kappa Alpha fraternity brothers in Confederate uniforms for the Old South Ball. I am first on the left in the middle row.*

*53. The KAs in uniforms and the girls in hoop skirts in front of Macon's historic Hay House.*

*54. The Macon Coliseum was completely full of people and candidates for graduation had taken their places. Later, when President Godsey presented my diploma, everyone in the Coliseum stood and applauded.*

*55. Mercer University President Kirby Godsey hands me my diploma and congratulates me.*

*56. This is Deryl Hoyal in the swing with me. I worked with her at the United Cerebral Palsy Center.*

*57. A great friend, Patsy Fried, always clowning around and making me laugh.*

*58. Three Kappa Alpha fraternity brothers—Daddy and me with famous author and our friend Dr. Ferrol "Sambo" Sams.*

*59. The Fire Administration Building where I work.*

*60. Fire chiefs Jim Hinson, Jim Hartley, and Marvin Riggins congratulate me at lunch. We were celebrating my attaining a permanent job with the City of Macon at the Fire Department Administration Headquarters. My parents look on.*

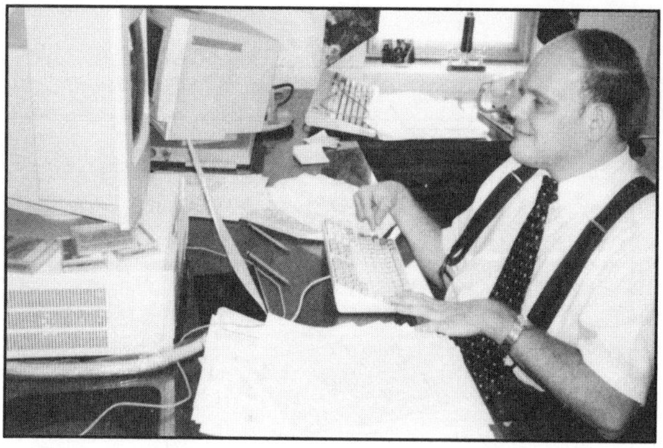

*61. Here I am at work at my computer at the Fire Administration Headquarters of the Macon/Bibb County Fire Department.*

# Chapter 1

## *My "Specialty"*

I have cerebral palsy, which affects all the muscles in my body. I can walk unassisted, but very slowly. Holding onto a rail, the side of a car, someone's arm, or a shopping cart, speeds me up greatly. Since my mouth and tongue are affected, my speech is often hard to understand, especially on the telephone. I can type about twenty-five words a minute, but am unable to go faster.

But just because I am handicapped in this manner, I do not feel I am a "special" person. People should not make a fuss over me. I like to do things for myself and to be as independent as possible. But sometimes others do not know this, and they try to help me when I do not need it.

For instance, if someone opens a door for me, I say, "Thank you," even though I can open it myself.

Because I cannot do some things as well as other people, I try even harder to do the things I can do. I have always enjoyed reading, writing, and schoolwork. Writing this book has been a real pleasure for me.

I like people best. I want lots of friends and things to do. My church, and the activities of the youth group there, have been a big part of my life. Along the way I have made hundreds of friends—fat ones, thin ones, short ones, tall ones—at school, at church, at Scouts, at camps, among my therapists and doctors, and elsewhere.

I remain grateful to my family and friends for their love and support during my upbringing and after reaching adulthood. I appreciate the patient help and care given me by many teachers, therapists, and other professional people. My church friends and pastors and the staff there have been some of my strongest supporters. I am especially thankful to those who gave me a chance when others could not or would not.

God has been good to me, to let me lead a near-normal life. I have seen many people more disabled than I am. I look at some of them and think how lucky I am.

# Chapter 2

# *My (Different) Beginnings*

I entered this world in an unusual way. Of course, I do not remember it. But from what my parents have told me, the events surrounding my birth were dramatic and frantic. It happened on October 9, 1958, in Macon, Georgia, a city of 150,000 people, about eighty-five miles south of Atlanta.

My mother was in the labor room of the city's main hospital with her fourth pregnancy and having light labor contractions. All indications were that everything would be routine. After all, she had had no problem delivering her three previous children, and there had been no trouble during this pregnancy. Not only that, it was early in the morning, when all the doctors were in the hospital. Two of mother's obstetricians were near by. My own father, a family practice physician himself, was in the hospital checking on his patients. He visited mother, and chatted with her doctors. As it appeared the baby was not coming any time soon, he then went elsewhere in the hospital, continuing to make his rounds.

Then, without warning, something went greatly wrong—the umbilical cord came out of mother's body! This is called prolapse of the cord. That was a huge emergency, as the blood flow in the cord got squeezed off and I was getting no oxygen.

One of the doctors, who was right there when it happened, screamed for aid from his doctor associate and from the nurses. They wasted no time. Mother was rushed down the hall to the obstetrical emergency operating room, a hastily called anesthetist put her to sleep, and they cut me out.

Meanwhile, my father had finished his hospital rounds, came back to the labor room, and wondered why mother still was not there. He found her in the operating room, just as I was being delivered by Caesarian section. The operating surgeon handed me to my father.

But I was not breathing or showing signs of life. My father and the second obstetrician worked very hard on me, giving me oxygen, artificial respiration, putting in an endotracheal tube, and trying to get me going. After about forty-five minutes I was breathing on my own and making weak noises. A pediatrician, investigating the disturbance, then came in and took over.

I was under oxygen in a bassinet in the nursery for three days. Fortunately, I could suck and drink from a bottle, and had no further trouble breathing. But my body and limbs were very weak. Even in this early stage the doctors feared the long period I had gone without oxygen might have damaged me.

MaMa Daniel, my wonderful grandmother on my mother's side, was at home recovering from a major heart attack at this time. No one had told her of my difficult birth, being afraid such news might give her another heart attack and kill her. So, on the way home from the hospital mother took me by MaMa Daniel's so she could see me. They tell me that she inspected me carefully, and must have been reassured by my normal appearance.

# Chapter 3

## *Getting Started*

Over the first year or so my development was abnormally slow. When I was twenty months old I was examined by Dr. Robert Bennett at his world-famous polio institute in Warm Springs, Georgia, where President Franklin D. Roosevelt had been treated. Dr. Bennett confirmed what had been suspected by all my Macon doctors, that I had cerebral palsy, but of the athetoid type. Most cerebral palsy is primarily of the spastic, or tight muscle, type. With athetoid cerebral palsy, the trouble is more with limpness and weakness of the muscles, poor balance, and sometimes with involuntary movements. Dr. Bennett gave me several recommendations, including a prescription for special shoes, and he suggested that I go to the Macon Cerebral Palsy center.

I got the special shoes, and mother started taking me to the Cerebral Palsy center, where I stayed a few hours every week day. At the center I received one-half hour of physical therapy and one-half hour of occupational therapy daily. The registered physical therapist there was Mr. William R. Burgamy, a great person. A little later Mr. Burgamy left the CP center and opened a private office downtown. For a while I continued going to the CP center, from which every day a small school bus would take those needing therapy from the center to Mr. Burgamy's office. A little later I started going from my home to his office as a private patient.

Mr. Burgamy began working with me when I was two years old, and I continued physical therapy with him at least three times a week until I was fourteen! One of the earliest exercises was for me to try to walk while holding on to parallel bars at his office. One of Daddy's patients made a set of parallel bars for me to practice on at home. Mr. Burgamy helped me more than any other single therapist.

At age two I went to a Macon orthopedist, and I would go to him periodically for the next several years. He recommended that I practice walking following footprints painted or pasted on the floor, wear weighted shoes, and start wearing short leg braces. He also suggested that I see Dr. Winthrop Phelps, a well-known orthopedic surgeon in Baltimore, Maryland. He was affiliated with Johns Hopkins University and was an authority on cerebral palsy, having written much on the subject.

## Chapter 4

# *Baltimore Bound*

Although I went to Dr. Phelps in Baltimore on four occasions at six- to twelve-month intervals, I remember little of this, except that I had to climb several flights of stairs in an old, dark building. In September 1961, my parents took me by train for my first visit there. After evaluating and examining me, Dr. Phelps agreed with my local orthopedist that I should start wearing short leg braces and special weighted shoes. Back in Macon, we had the braces and shoes made to specifications, and soon I had braces on both legs from just below the knees down to my feet. On Dr. Phelps's recommendation, I had my hearing checked at the Atlanta Speech and Hearing School, and it was normal.

My second visit to Dr. Phelps took place in the Spring of 1962. This time the whole family went along in the station wagon. It was spring holidays at school, so we combined the trip to the doctor with a short family vacation in Washington, D.C. But the most memorable event of this trip took place on the way up, at the Rip Van Winkle Motel in Sanford, North Carolina, where I nearly died of an acute asthma attack in the middle of the night. It was difficult for my father to find a pharmacist to open up his drugstore so late at night, but he finally did. The pharmacist went to his store and made up a special medicine on Daddy's prescription. After getting this medicine I eventually started breathing easier, but I am told there were some anxious moments for my family. I continued having asthma attacks of varying severity on and off until puberty, when the attacks disappeared.

We spent several days in Washington seeing the sights. I do not remember this incident, but I am told that my sister Beverly became very excited in the White House when she saw what she thought was Caroline Kennedy's sweater, initialed "C.K.," hanging on a hook.

Then we went to Baltimore for my appointment with Dr. Phelps. This time he ordered longer leg braces, high up on my thighs, and he recommended that I wear a hockey helmet during all waking hours, to protect my head from falls. Shortly back home, I found myself wearing the helmet and the long leg braces.

The initial train trip to Baltimore, then the long drive by car, taught us this was not the way to go so far. On my last two visits, Daddy and I went by airplane. This was much quicker, but was very hectic, and a Macon-Baltimore-Macon air trip would go something like this.

My father would drive us to Atlanta, and we would leave our car in the air terminal parking and hurry into the Atlanta airport to catch the 10:10 a.m. flight. In addition to having to look after me, Daddy would also have to carry a suitcase for my braces and a fold-up stroller. The flight from Atlanta to Washington National Airport would take about an hour and a half. At Washington airport daddy would immediately rent a car at the airport front entrance, then we would race across the city, stopping for a quick lunch. Then we would speed up the Baltimore-Washington Expressway. By the time we reached south Baltimore it would already be 2:00 p.m., the time of our appointment, so Daddy would have to go to a pay phone and call Dr. Phelps's office to tell him that we were running late. About 2:30 p.m. we would get to his office in north Baltimore.

Dr. Phelps would see me soon after we arrived. He was very nice and knowledgeable, and would examine me thoroughly. About 4:00 p.m. or later we would leave his office, get in the rented car, and drive back to Washington. But due to peculiarities in airline scheduling, we would always have to go about forty miles west of Washington, to Dulles Airport in Virginia, to fly back to Atlanta. After flying back and getting on the ground in Atlanta, we would have to drive back to Macon. This was a lot to do in one day.

Once, coming back, the Eastern Airlines plane was so crowded in the coach section that I had to ride the whole way back in Daddy's lap, in the middle seat of a three-seat row. We had two full-fare tickets but, in spite of pleading with the stewardess who would come through, we never got two seats. But the pilot of this flight must have been trying to make up time for being late, as the heavily loaded plane flew from Washington to Atlanta in exactly sixty minutes! In spite of that, the rest of my family, waiting in Atlanta, was really worried because we were so late.

On my third visit to Dr. Phelps, he extended the bracing to my waist. On the fourth visit he talked about extending the braces to include my chest and head.

That scared us, so we quit going to Baltimore. My physical therapist, Mr. Burgamy, had always disagreed with Dr. Phelps's prescription for more and more bracing. Later, when all my braces were taken off on another doctor's recommendation, my leg muscles had almost entirely shriveled away. It took years and years of therapy for the muscles to be built back up big and strong, as they are now.

## Chapter 5

# *My Family*

I have two older brothers, David and Clark, and an older sister, Beverly. David is a newspaper editor, and he has helped me tremendously on this book. Beverly works for a capital investment company. Clark is a property tax and real estate appraiser and consultant. David and Beverly live in Atlanta, and Clark lives in Florida. I have a nephew, Beverly's son Daniel, and a niece, Clark's daughter Christina or Christy, and a step-grandmother named Clariece, who lives in Columbus, Georgia. I have three aunts and three uncles. Uncle Joe and Aunt Mary Helen Daniel live in Macon. Uncle Joe is mother's brother, and is a physician like my father. My father's sister Lillian, whom I call Aunt Lil, is a writer and is married to Jack Watt, a Ph.D., who is a retired professor from the University of Texas and Georgia Tech. Uncle Jack taught mechanical engineering and health systems engineering. He is a nationally known expert on refrigeration, and has written the standard textbook on evaporative cooling. Aunt Lil and Uncle Jack live in Atlanta.

My other uncle, my father's brother Harold, is also a Ph.D. and an author. He is retired from teaching history at Radford University, in Radford, Virginia. He is married to my Aunt Betty. They live in Durham, North Carolina. My mother's sister, Aunt Elizabeth, died in 1985, and her husband, Uncle Tag, a Georgia Tech graduate and an engineer, died in 1990. Altogether my aunts and uncles have produced thirteen cousins for me.

One of my earliest memories is of playing with wooden blocks my parents had given me for Christmas. I built tall towers and David took pictures of these structures. There were many other toys in the house I enjoyed playing with, but most of all I liked playing outside with my brothers, my sister, and with the neighboring children. We lived in a neighborhood called Thornwood. Another doctor, Dr. Leonard Campbell, and his wife lived next door. Mother and Fil Campbell were very good friends.

Another household of friends several doors down the street was that of Mr. and Mrs. Lester Moore. My sister Beverly was so attached to that family that she nearly lived down there with their two girls. The youngest child in that family, Michael, and I were about the same age, and played together all the time. I remember one special day when Michael and I played in the sandbox in the back yard. The day was special because this was the day mother took Beverly and her girlfriend to see the Beatles in concert in Atlanta.

We had a female dachshund we called "Schatzie Hamburger." Mother's cousin John McCullough knew all about dogs and loved dachshunds. When we asked him what he would suggest we name our dog, he said, "Schatzie."

Dachshunds originated in Germany, and John said this name meant "sweetheart" in German. David tried to think of something else with a German connotation. Since dachshunds are shaped like wieners, which reminds one of hamburgers, we ended up calling her both names, "Schatzie Hamburger."

Schatzie thought her job in life was to follow me around and protect me, and this she did for many years, paying little attention to anyone else, even Mother, who fed her. Soon after Schatzie died in December 1970 we got a collie puppy named "Caesar." Six weeks later veterinarian Dr. Mack Butler and his wife Edith, my cousin, gave us a black miniature poodle puppy. We named him "Beauregard" and called him "Beau." Beau and Caesar were really cute growing up together. After a few years, however, Caesar began chasing cars and people, so we had to give him away to some friends who lived in the country.

Another interesting set of pets we had for awhile were the fish that my brother Clark collected. He set up an aquarium in the breakfast room. The biggest fish in the tank was an Oscar fish, so we named him "Oscar." The second biggest fish was named "Jack Dempsey." Oscar had almost as much personality as a dog. He would eat all the other fish and eventually grew to be huge—about a foot long!

Clark was a very outdoor type boy and loved to play in the creek and explore the woods near our house. He also liked to play pranks. Once he and some other boys were out shooting firecrackers, which is illegal in Macon. A policeman caught Clark and dragged him to our house.

The policeman asked my mother, "Is this your son?"

"Yes," she answered.

I was scared and crying. I had never seen anyone arrested. The policeman took Clark and the other boys down to the police station, but they let them off after a warning.

A loving person in our family was our maid and cook Lucille ("Cille") Tillman. When I was young, she strolled me to the Rosa Taylor School playground every afternoon to watch the children. She stayed night and day with me and my brothers and sister when my parents were away on any medical trip. Cille was fun and sweet all the eighteen years she worked for us. We were sad when she was in an automobile wreck, broke her hip, and later had to leave us. Mother never found another person to help her as loyal as Cille.

## Chapter 6

# *Special Education, Therapies, and Camps*

Due to my cerebral palsy my speech has always been bad, and over the years I have had many speech therapists and speech pathologists. My first speech teacher, when I was four, was Mrs. Wilmoth Clinard. She lived on our street and came to my house to give me therapy. She told us about the Tinsley School of Special Education, a public school in the Bibb County school system, which was located on Pierce Avenue, near our home. Mrs. Clinard suggested that we go to see Mrs. Dorothy Poythress, the head of this school, about the possibility that I might go there.

In June 1963 my parents and I went to see Mrs. Poythress. We carried extensive records, and she questioned me. She kindly said I should start going to this school in September! This was great good fortune to be allowed to enter this school, as in all of Bibb County there was only one nine-to-twelve-pupil class for beginning students like me, who were called "multihandicapped." There was one similar upper class for the multihandicapped at this same school, into which those in the lower class were usually promoted after several years. At this special school, in addition to the upper and lower classes for the multihandicapped, there were classes for the hearing impaired. This special school was located behind the regular Tinsley Elementary School, and was connected to it by a covered walk. The mentally retarded and other mentally handicapped students of Bibb County went to other schools in the public school system.

In September 1963, when I was not quite five years old, I entered Mrs. Riley's beginning class at the T. D. Tinsley School of Special Education. The first few days I cried and cried, but after about two weeks I became happy and eager to learn. Mrs. Carolyn Riley, who taught these younger children, instructed me in reading, writing, adding, and in working on my own. She also taught me to hang up my coat and to keep my papers and supplies in order. Mrs. Riley worked hard with me, teaching me new things day after day.

Only eight days after entering this class I had a bad attack of asthma, and had to be in the Macon Hospital for two days. Beverly felt so sorry for me she climbed in the oxygen tent with me! After discharge, I went right back to school, and Mrs. Riley started right back working with me.

At this school I made many friends. Janie was the maid, and C. J. James was the janitor and the man in charge of getting the children into the building (many had to be lifted and carried) and into class. James and I became very good friends. He called me "Doc," because my father is a doctor. He and Stuart, a classmate, and I would laugh and joke together. We had a great time. James is now dead.

In the summer of 1964 I went back to the Cerebral Palsy center for two months. I did not enjoy this very much. First, it was a long drive from my home. Then, while there, although we did make some things with our hands at a table, at other times we were idle.

When almost six, I started my second year in Mrs. Riley's class. The school now provided me with an occupational therapist, who started some exercises on my legs.

We had quit going to Dr. Phelps in Baltimore, but heard about another expert in nearby Atlanta, the orthopedic surgeon Dr. Joseph Dimon III. I was eight years old when I first went to see him in January 1967.

He said, "Braces off!"

So my father started taking the braces off slowly. When he did, my leg muscles had shrunk even further. At once Mr. Burgamy, back in Macon, started even more intensive physical therapy than I had been getting. I would sit on a table with my legs hanging down, and he would put weights on my feet. Then he would make me raise each weighted leg straight out many times. I worked extremely hard on strengthening my legs for many years. Eventually I was able not only to make the muscles come back in size, but to become really strong, both in the arms and legs. Then I was able to walk in the house, and later in the yard, with crutches onto which sandbags had been taped at the bottoms, but with no braces. I was eight years old before I could walk everywhere unassisted with these crutches.

After being in Mrs. Riley's lower special education multihandicapped class for four years, I was promoted to Mrs. Exie Williams's upper special education class at the same school. She taught me more difficult things, such as the multiplication tables, spelling, harder reading and writing, a little more arithmetic, and social things such as how to make friends with everybody—I had always done that anyway! The first year I was in Mrs. Williams's class I was the youngest student in the class. I had loved Mrs. Riley's class so much I had hated to leave it, but I soon learned to love Mrs. Williams's class just as much. I will always have fond memories of Mrs. Riley and Mrs. Williams, both of whom worked so hard with me, and who were so caring.

Mrs. Williams is a short lady, but she knew her business and what she was supposed to do. My first year in Mrs. Williams's class was a hard time for me, as it was different from what I had been doing for four years in Mrs. Riley's class. Mrs. Williams was very good to me, though, and helped me with my reading, on my workbooks, and on my talking.

I had my hearing checked again at the Central Georgia Speech and Hearing Center in Macon. My hearing was all right, but my speech was not good. So I started taking speech lessons from Mr. Frank Rhodes at the center. We worked on the sounds *g, s, b, f, v, ch, sh,* and more. I also took additional speech therapy from the speech therapist at Tinsley school. I worked very hard on my speech, trying to improve it so people would understand me better.

One of the best things that happened to me at Tinsley was that I learned to type. When I was nine, the occupational therapist, the Easter Seal lady Mrs. Theo Fisher, decided to see if she could teach any of the Tinsley students to type. She started with two girls and me. The girls soon dropped out, but I took to it like a duck takes to water.

Easter Seal furnished the school with a large IBM electric typewriter. It had a special metal plate attached to the keyboard, with holes for the keys. The solid plate between the keys would keep the fingers of handicapped students from going down between the keys. Mrs. Fisher, from the beginning, insisted that all the keys on the typewriter be completely covered up with glued-on patches! This, of course, was to force the typist to memorize the keys. It really worked! To help with the covered keys there was a large diagram of the keyboard on the wall in front of the typewriter at school. I bought a typewriter just like the one at school to practice on at home. I also kept a huge keyboard poster on my wall at home, just above the typewriter. After several years of typing, I no longer needed the metal plate, but I kept the keys covered for about ten years.

In the summer of 1969 I went to Camp Easter Seal at a Georgia state park, Magnolia Springs. My counselor was Mike Thompson. Mike and I worked together and played together for two weeks. I was ten years old then, and I was homesick and cried a lot, because it was my first time away from home. I remember the camp was hilly and rocky, but there were a lot of fun things to do like swimming, horseback riding, arts and crafts, sitting around campfires, and much more.

That summer my parents had sold our house on Thornwood Drive, and had bought a house on Hillandale Circle. We had to be out of our old house by July first, but our new house was not vacated. So my family had to split up. One of my brothers, Clark, went and stayed with Uncle Joe and Aunt Mary Helen. My older brother David went over to my grandparents' and stayed there. My sister Beverly, my father, my mother, and I stayed in a rented, very small cabin at the Pinebrook Inn in Macon. During July and August we ran across the city for six weeks, until our new house was ready to be moved into. After moving, we had to paint the inside and outside, put on a new roof, put down some new tile in the kitchen, and make other repairs.

The first two years in Mrs. Williams's class seemed to have gone by rapidly. In the Fall of 1969 I started back in Mrs. Williams's class for my third year with her, and for my seventh year at the Tinsley School of Special Education. Mrs. Williams gave me spelling words to learn every week, and she would test me on this every Friday. She also gave me folder work to do, when she was working with other pupils.

That year in November I walked clear across thc house without a crutch for the first time! I had been walking a little at Mr. Burgamy's office, but this was the first time I had done it at home.

In the Summer of 1970 I went to Easter Seal camp again, this time at Fort Yargo State Park near Winder, Georgia, for twelve days. Several of my classmates from Tinsley also went to this camp. Every evening we had a program, including a hillbilly night, a Halloween night, and, on the last evening, an awards night. I won the Most Popular Camper award.

# Chapter 7

## *Art and Amy Bishop*

I was a young teenager when we got a new preacher. In June 1971 a young Methodist minister named Rev. Arthur L. Bishop came and took the job of Minister of Education and Youth at the church. Art and I soon became good friends. We joked together and played together.

When he first came to Macon Art was single, but he soon began courting an out-of-town girl named Amy. For months Amy came to our church every Sunday. In the Summer of 1972 Art and Amy were married in a church at St. Simons Island, Georgia, Amy's home. Shortly after they were married Amy was appointed director of the children's choir at our church here in Macon. She encouraged me to join the choir and hum the tunes, and I did.

I had gone to Riverside United Methodist Church all my life and was fairly active. But I did not join the church until I was thirteen, on March 26, 1972. After joining, and with Art and Amy doing so many programs, I became very involved with the youth in the UMYF (United Methodist Youth Fellowship.) I have remained active with the youth ever since, being a counselor with them since I became an adult.

At first we met in the scout hut in the back of the church's lot. Every Sunday one of the mothers would fix supper for everyone. The menu would be simple, the food consisting of something like hot dogs, hamburgers, pizza, chili, or barbecue. We had many activities in the youth program, and more and more young people came. Soon twenty-five or thirty boys and girls were attending every week.

Amy helped Art with everything, but her main work was with the youth choir and with the children's choir. Amy was a great choir director, and our youth choir put on the program of Christmas music for the church in 1972.

I continued being very busy with the youth group. Every Sunday evening after supper and fellowship we broke up into small groups. The attendance kept growing. By about six months after Art's arrival forty or so would come every week.

There were many other special activities and trips. In the summer of 1973 Art, Amy, and I, and others in the youth group went on a Monday-to-Saturday camp. My cousin Lyn Gibson, from another church, also went. Art was my counselor. One day Art, Amy, Amy's cousin Cisty Cannon, and I visited a nearby attraction called Land of the Ratman. This was in an old, vacant, dilapidated house, infested with rats and filled with cobwebs and dirt.

One night we went to a gospel movie at a local theater. It was a Billy Graham movie called *Time to Run*. After the show, when the call was made, some of us went up to the front of the theater to "find Christ." Doug Pyles and I were in the group that went forward. One of the movie employees gave out information on the film.

One Saturday the UMYF, the Bishop's, Amy's sister Kim, and I went to Six Flags Over Georgia near Atlanta. Since I walk so slowly, before leaving I had borrowed a wheelchair from the T. D. Tinsley Special Education Department. We left Macon on a bus about 8:00 a.m. and got inside the gate there about 10:00 a.m. The wheelchair was too big for the gate, so Art and I went through the police door. Everyone wanted to stay with me, hoping he could ride in the wheelchair and get this special treatment.

But Art said, "No one except Gary can ride in that wheelchair!"

So Art, Cisty Cannon, and I stayed together.

When the workers saw that I was in a wheelchair they would say, "Just push in through the exits."

In this manner we did more than anyone else. And it "paid off" to be in a wheelchair.

About a year after they married, Art and Amy had a baby boy they named Lanny.

The day after the Six Flags visit I found out that the South Georgia Methodist Conference had decided that Art should have his own church, and he was assigned to the only Methodist church in Putney, Georgia. He would have to move in a week! I was sad that my youth director, who had done so much for the church, with its youth program, and who had been so wonderful to me, would be leaving so soon. The last Sunday Art was here, in the regular main church service, the youth gave him a present. Art was a good leader and everybody was crazy about him. We were all unhappy that he had to go away.

Several weeks after they moved to Putney, my parents and I stopped by their new home to visit them. We were on our way to a vacation at the beach. They were very glad to see us.

In December 1974 Art and Amy had another baby boy named Matthew, which they called Matt. About a month after Matt was born Art and Amy and the two boys came back to Macon for Robert Pyles's fifteenth birthday, and I was able to see them.

Today Art and Amy are living in Columbus, Georgia, where he is associated with a church. They now have been blessed with three sons.

# Chapter 8

## *Don Clarke*

In June 1974 another Methodist minister named Donald B. Clarke came to take the job of Minister of Education and Youth at our church. The first time I met Don I was doing yard work at the church. Three days a week my job was to pick up beer cans, paper, cups, bottles, and old homework. Once I even found a full bottle of beer.

One day, just before Art Bishop left, I saw Art and a young, good-looking man coming toward me.

Art said to me, "Gary, I want you to meet the new Youth Director who will be taking my place, Don Clarke."

Six days after he arrived, all the youth met Don during Sunday School. That night Don was still afraid, so we cheered him up with a cake and a party after church. About three days later he called a two-evening meeting to plan the summer. After the first night's meeting we went to get a pizza at a local restaurant. The meeting the next night was even better, and everybody seemed to like Don.

A few weeks later my grandfather, Rev. D. G. Mann, came to my home and said, "I wonder if Don Clarke is kin to you. Maybe fifteenth or sixteenth cousin, but maybe he is kin in some way."

Clark (without the "e") was the maiden name of PaPa's wife and my grandmother, Gertrude. But we never found out whether he was kin to us on Gertrude's side.

Just about the time Don got to Riverside, my family went on a vacation. When we got back, Don had already really taken over the Riverside United Methodist youth group. Boy, did he move in fast! Don had already started working hard, was bringing more people to Riverside

UMYF, and was planning lots of things to do and fun for everyone. Art had been a good Youth Director, but he was married and they had a baby boy, and he could not spend as much time with the youth as Don, a bachelor then, could.

Don had us do so many things it was as if a whirlwind had stirred up the youth. Everybody loved Don, and the group kept growing, to more than one hundred.

One time the youth group went to eat a seafood supper at High Falls State Park. After eating, we all went down to the big and beautiful falls. It gave me a great sense of peace to see that wonder of nature.

In November of 1974 my friend Stuart Evans, now living in Savannah, visited back in Macon and came to see me. He also went to a campfire with our youth group. He was crazy about Don, and enjoyed seeing some of his former friends.

Don kept on working with the youth, and doing more and more things. We continued to get crowds of youngsters. We had all sorts of activities and projects, but we had a lot of fun.

In April 1975 we went to Henderson Settlement near Frakes, Kentucky (population fifty). It was run by the United Methodist Church. We were there the first weekend of the month. We arrived about 1:45 a.m. That same morning we got up at 7:00 a.m. and started to work at the settlement. The work gave me a good feeling to help people who are in need.

In July 1975 Don, the youth, and I went to Six Flags Over Georgia again. As before, I took the wheelchair. I rode on many rides, including the Scream Machine, the world's largest roller coaster at that time. Another thing we did that summer month was to go to Stone Mountain, Georgia. I was impressed by the huge faces of Robert E. Lee, Stonewall Jackson, and Jefferson Davis. The skylift to the top of Stone Mountain was scary but was something to remember.

In November 1975 I was getting my courses set up for school. One of my courses was Government. My new government teacher was Terry Sark, a graduate of Asbury College in Kentucky, a religious institution. In addition to being a teacher, he was a church choir director.

Since Don was also a graduate of Asbury, I asked him, "One of my teachers, who is also a choir director, was in college with you. Guess who?"

Don immediately replied, "Terry Sark!"

Don was so busy with his work it would seem he would not have time for anything else. But, during his stay at Riverside, he managed to find, fall in love with, and marry a nice and likable young lady named Elaine DuMond.

His marriage did not slow him down, and we often have more than a hundred teenagers to come on Sunday nights or for weeknight activities. But finally the Georgia Methodist Conference did the same to Don as it had to Art. It decided he needed a church of his own. He was transferred away, to be the pastor of a small chuch near Athens, Georgia. We were all sad to see him leave. But since then we have continued to get a series of good ministers of youth at our church.

Don and Elaine have two children. Unfortunately, I have been able to see them only a few times since they left Macon.

## Chapter 9

# *Kevin and Nancy Murphy*

On August 10, 1974, my first cousin got married at Riverside United Methodist Church, my church. During the wedding I discovered a tall young man and his wife, Kevin and Nancy Murphy. They were singing in the wedding. Kevin was a Mercer student taking religious courses. Nancy was studying music at Mercer, too.

The next week was Youth Week at Riverside, and I was pleasantly surprised to find that Kevin and Nancy were the leaders. I went three out of the five times. I really got to know them. The times I went we had a blind walk, land sales, and Bible stories to act out.

A youth worker named Lynn Skene started a folk singing group at the church. There were four lead singers, and twenty-four boys and girls, including me, sang in the background, in the choir loft. The group was called the "Good News Express."

About a month later, on a Wednesday afternoon, I went to a church meeting. It was decided that a youth choir, in addition to the folk group, should be formed. The choir was founded and named "Riverside Youth Choir." At once we started working, under Kevin's and Nancy's direction, on music from the musical "I Looked for Love."

In November 1974 we sang three songs on the same program as "The Archers" from Burbank, California, who had come to our church. The star sang the last song holding my hand.

In January 1975 we first performed "I Looked for Love" at Riverside church. Later we performed for other churches and for a nursing home in Macon.

About two weeks later Kevin started to have a fellowship evening every Saturday night at his home. We sang, played games, and had prayer circles and refreshments. Kevin told us about growing up in New York City.

We started working on the musical "He Is Alive." It was harder music from six music books. One song was written and sung by a good friend of mine and a member of the choir. Another song was sung by two students from Wesleyan College in Macon.

In May 1975 we went on our choir tour to Eastman, Savannah, Savannah Beach, and Reynolds in Georgia. Don Clarke was the youth leader, but Kevin and Nancy were in charge of the music. When we got to Savannah Beach we found William Stuart Evans III, my old friend, who now lived in Savannah. After finding Stuart, we started setting up for a concert on the beach that Saturday afternoon, to try to drum up interest in our concert that night in a chapel at Savannah Beach.

When the program that night was about to start, we were all tired and fussy, and the bass player had gone home sick. Also there were only a handful of people in the audience. So we went in a back room of the church, joined hands in a prayer circle, and prayed for a successful evening. And a miracle occurred. When we went out to do the program about five minutes later the pews were packed full of people, though no additional cars were noted parked outside! Maybe all these people were angels. And we gave one of our best concerts.

The next day, Sunday, we sang at the morning service at a Methodist Church on Skidaway Island nearby; then we went to Reynolds, Georgia, for the last concert on Sunday night, then home.

A little later Kevin and Nancy started working on an album. They taped it, and it was ready in July of that year. I bought one and it was great.

Today Kevin and Nancy are living in Tennessee. Kevin is working for an insurance company and singing on the side.

## Chapter 10

# *Reece and Onie Turrentine*

In the summer of 1972 a new preacher took the job as the head minister of Riverside United Methodist Church. My mother was on the committee to fix up the home for the family. The couple finally arrived. Their names were Reece and Onie Turrentine, and they had two children named Mike and Linda. Reece was a graduate of Emory University in Atlanta. He was also a good camper and canoeist. The Turrentines came from Fort Valley, Georgia.

In his first sermon at Riverside, Reece said, "If you can't remember Turrentine, just remember that it sounds like turpentine, and turpentine is sap—so if you just remember 'sap,' you should not have any trouble."

Mike was a mischievous big boy. He and Reece rode motorcycles all the time. One time I wrote Mike a letter and told him he owed me eight cents for the stamp. I wrote him another letter and told him all about the books I had copied to practice typing.

The Turrentines had a dog named Harry, who was a very bright dog in most ways, but he would chase skunks, and this would make him smell bad!

Reece also painted pictures. When my mother and I went over to the parsonage we saw a picture he had painted of a boat. It was very good. In his office were more pictures he had done. One was of the earth. Another picture in his office was an optical illusion. At first it looked like faces, but with a dim light the picture turned into the face of God.

Reece and I grew to be good friends, and he was also a good friend of my grandfather's, Rev. David G. Mann, who was then minister of evangelism at Riverside.

While Reece was our pastor my sister Beverly was married in Riverside United Methodist Church. My grandfather, PaPa Mann, helped him perform the ceremony.

Reece was very popular with our church members, so much so that he was allowed to stay here much longer than the Methodist conference usually allows a preacher to remain in one place. Usually Methodist preachers are moved about every four to six years, but Reece was allowed to stay here for nine years, from 1972 to 1981. Many people thought Reece was the best preacher they had ever heard.

Just about everybody liked Reece and Onie. Onie taught school full time, so she could not do many weekday activities at the church, but she was well liked. Reece was so proud of the beautiful new sanctuary, which was finished during his tenure, that he rode with the workmen on a platform hanging from a crane to put the steeple on top of the bell tower, the final act of the builders.

In June 1981 Reece and Onie moved to Atlanta. Reece took off a year to work as a writer for a magazine. Today he is one of the ministers for the largest Methodist church in Atlanta.

# Chapter 11

## *The One and Only William Stuart Evans III*

I first met William Stuart Evans III in the fall of 1963, when I started going to the T. D. Tinsley School of Special Education. Everyone called him Stuart. The first teacher he and I had together was Mrs. Carolyn Riley. Stuart and I became great friends. We went to school together and played together.

Stuart was a comedian. One day my Aunt Elizabeth picked up Stuart and me from school. As Stuart was getting into the car he asked her, "May I see your driver's license?"

Stuart lived in Ingleside in Macon. I lived about two miles from him, on Thornwood Drive near Rosa Taylor Elementary School. Stuart was over at my home often, and I was over at his a lot too. His favorite sandwich was bologna. When Stuart came over we would always ask, "Do you want a bologna sandwich?"

His answer would be, "I want a plate full."

Stuart and I began taking music from Mrs. Evelyn Gates. Mrs. Gates was a funny woman. She gave Stuart the name of "Stu-fish" and gave me the name "Slow Poke," after the song, because I was so slow. Mrs. Gates did not use the word "crutch;" she used the word "stick."

There were some volunteer workers at Tinsley, including Mrs. Patsy Fried, who came from the Red Cross. Mrs. Fried was a good friend to my mother and all of my family. Patsy Fried's job was to draw up the students' papers (including Stuart's and mine.) Patsy was fun and made everybody laugh. When she kissed Stuart, Stuart's face became red, real red!

In May 1964 Stuart and I went to our first picnic at Patsy's home, to eat hamburgers and to ride the horse that her husband E. J. put us on. Patsy has been giving this picnic annually at her house for about thirty years. She invites all the students and teachers at the Tinsley Special Education School. It is a funny thing, but in all those years, and even though it is during our rainy season, her picnic has never been rained out.

My brother Clark got into play battles with Stuart and me. We fought with Clark all the time. I do not think Stuart or I won once out of a thousand fights and battles. We were at each other for at least ten years.

Mrs. Riley had a dog named Spot—because it had black spots all over. Spot followed Mrs. Riley to school every morning for many years, and would lie down in the classroom all day long. Spot finally died of old age.

James, the handyman and janitor, was everybody's favorite, especially Stuart's and mine. I remember we had some far out and good times together. Like when we went over to Patsy Fried's every year, Stuart and I tried to eat more hamburgers than James.

One year Stuart, several classmates and I, along with Mrs. Exie Williams's class, were on T.V., on Doris Martin's show. I played a little teapot and Stuart played a teddy bear. We put on this play twice: the first time Stuart was out of town; the second time he was there—and Mrs. Riley had to dance! The play was taped for T.V. Both Mrs. Riley and Mrs. Williams are now retired. Mrs. Gates is also retired.

In the fall of 1967 Stuart and I went our separate ways. Stuart stayed in Mrs. Riley's class, while I went to Mrs. Williams's class. In this class there were only nine students, counting me. I made friends with the new students. The next few years Stuart slowly calmed down, but had at least seven years of heavy fun and jokes with James and me.

In the winter of 1972 Stuart and his family moved to Savannah, Georgia. I was very sad that my best friend was moving away. That meant I would have to get along without Stuart.

The years passed, but Stuart would come back to Macon occasionally to stay with relatives. When in town he would visit me. Stuart would always go back in Clark's room and play the pinball machine for hours. He went wild over it! He finally became better than I on the pinball machine, but I never told anyone.

Stuart came back to see me again in March 1974. While playing pinball he said, "Gary, I want you to go to camp with me in Southern Pines, North Carolina, this summer."

So in July of that year Stuart and I went to Camp Easter-N-the-Pines, North Carolina's Easter Seal camp at Southern Pines. My father and mother took Stuart and me up there. At camp we did all kinds of things, like riding horses, swimming, boat riding, and going to movies and dances. Stuart and I were in the same cabin.

In November 1974 Stuart discovered that I was in the youth group of Riverside United Methodist Church. He came back to Macon to visit, and met a lot of my friends at church. I think Craig and Doug Pyles were among Stuart's favorites. That summer Stuart came to a swimming party at my Uncle Joe's and Aunt Mary Helen's house in Macon. Some boys threw Doug into the water with all of his clothes on.

The first weekend in September 1975 I got a postcard from Stuart saying, "I am going to the Crippled Children's school in Jamestown, North Dakota."

But the card was from Bloomington, Minnesota. I thought it was a shame for Stuart to have to go that far away for a high school education. Surely there was a closer school for him, in Georgia or somewhere in the Southeast.

In January 1976 Stuart came back to Macon and visited me and gave me a bad time, while he played Clark's new pinball machine.

When he started playing the new machine he said, "This machine does not like me."

I had tried to get Doug, Craig, Don Clarke, and some others of our mutual friends to come over to my house to visit Stuart, but everyone was busy with other things. So none of them was able to come at that time. Stuart got better on pinball by late afternoon, and could play me a good game.

Thc ncxt month I wrotc Stuart and told him that Doug and Craig were moving from Macon to Charlotte, North Carolina.

Today Stuart in living in Savannah in his own apartment. I have visited him several times when I have gone to the Savannah area, but it has been a long time since I last saw this old friend.

# Chapter 12

## *Reverend David G. Mann*

David G. Mann's life of eighty-nine-plus years started in Jonesboro, Georgia, near Atlanta. A baby boy was born on August 20, 1887, and was named David Gilbert Mann. His father was David Alexander Mann, and his mother's maiden name was Anne Smith. David was the youngest child, and he had many brothers and sisters. But his favorite brother was Zack. Zack and David played together all the time. They played at the railroad, at the lake and ponds, at the circus, and in the countryside.

David G. Mann told some great stories about World War I, of meeting the Wright brothers at the circus, of the ministry, of old and new preacher friends, and of old-time days.

He joined the South Georgia Conference of the Methodist Church as a minister in 1910. After serving as a pastor of churches in several small south Georgia towns for less than ten years, the United States had gotten into World War I, and he joined the U. S. Army as a chaplain.

After induction into the Army, every month PaPa wrote a long letter to Rev. Rose, a minister friend. The letters started while Rev. Mann was in this country, but most of them were written from France to Dr. Rose here in the United States. All these letters have been saved, and have come into the possession of my family. Most of them were twenty to thirty handwritten pages long. I had the opportunity to type them up, and they were very interesting. Some of them dated back to 1917.

PaPa served in the Rainbow (57th) Division, which was in most of the big battles of World War I in Europe. At the end of the war the French government was so grateful for his extraordinary performance that it offered him a free term at the world-famous Sorbonne University in

Paris. He took them up on the offer, and made all A's, even though all the courses, of course, were taught in French, which he had never studied! PaPa was glad to get this additional education. But his wife (my sweet grandmother Gertrude) was not too happy about his staying overseas longer, as their first child, a daughter named Lillian, was born before he came home.

One of his stories I never shall forget was that when he was ordained, with his own eyes he saw Jesus. He told about this, for the first time to anybody, in his last sermon. That is the way I found out about it.

Over the years one of PaPa's greatest sources of enjoyment was the garden in his back yard. He planted a garden every year, and he grew okra, squash, tomatoes, radishes, butterbeans, and other things. When the crop came in he would always bring some of the fresh produce over to our house, and we would enjoy cooking and eating this good food.

He founded about fifteen new Methodist churches in the Middle Georgia area of Macon and Warner Robins (about eighteen miles from Macon). I do not know the names of all of them, but I know of a few around Macon. One I am familiar with is Shurlington United Methodist Church, which my friend Craig Pyles and one of my special education teachers formerly attended. PaPa also helped start Forest Hills and Bloomfield Methodist Churches, also Riverside, and many others.

My grandfather was very active as the minister of visitation, at my own church, Riverside United Methodist Church, long after his mandatory "retirement." In fact, PaPa Mann decided on the location for this new church, and saw that the Methodist authorities bought the land, and that the church got built. This was all approved by his district superintendent, Rev. Tom Whiting.

April 17, 1964, was observed as "Dave Mann Day" at Riverside, honoring him.

Several years after PaPa's wife Gertrude died, in October 1973 PaPa got a phone call from Miss Clariece Greer of Columbus, Georgia. She was visiting in Macon, and wanted to see PaPa at a friend's home here. So PaPa went to this home, and met again with this lady. It was the first time he had seen her in fifty years, when she had joined his Columbus church when she was a teenager.

After this meeting, PaPa continued seeing Clariece. In mid-November of that year he asked my folks if he could invite Clariece to our home for our annual big family Thanksgiving dinner. Of course we were glad to do this. We were delighted to find Clariece to be a nice, friendly, joyful, fast-talking, and funny lady. We all liked her. Thanksgiving night PaPa proposed to Clariece, and she accepted. She had never been married before.

In December 1973, the Sunday before Christmas, PaPa and Clariece were married at Riverside United Methodist Church. The wedding was unusual, as this couple was married during the regular Sunday morning church service. The service was performed by Rev. Reece Turrentine. I stood by Clariece's side throughout the ceremony. PaPa's daughter Lillian with her husband Jack and PaPa's other son Harold with his wife Betty had all come from out of town for this important event.

Every Sunday after church Clariece and PaPa, my mother, my father, and I, went to the Ramada Inn to eat lunch. All the staff in the lunchroom became very friendly with us.

In his last years PaPa was the oldest remaining preacher in the South Georgia Conference of the United Methodist Church. Every June he continued to go to the week-long South Georgia Conference meeting in Macon, which had been a big event for him all his life.

In May 1976 PaPa and Clariece went to Hawaii for eight days, and they enjoyed the trip immensely, although PaPa became very ill on the way home. They brought me back a fancy shirt, and some rock from the volcano on the big island of Hawaii.

To me, in his later years, every day Brother Dave seemed to grow not older, but younger. I loved him, and I am glad that he was my grandfather, and that Clariece is my step-grandmother.

PaPa died on Saturday, June 25th, 1977. It was the saddest day of my life. He was almost ninety years old. But even though he was old, it was hard for me to accept his death. I could not stop crying, and felt I would be unhappy forever. I was eighteen years old at the time. PaPa Mann had been my friend, my beloved grandparent, and he had the greatest influence on my life. My dream was to be just like him, and to be a preacher too.

Two days after his death there was a big funeral in Riverside United Methodist Church, conducted by three ministers. PaPa would have been ninety years old in seven weeks.

Many times he had said to me, as I was growing up, "I'm going to live to be ninety, or maybe even a hundred."

His not quite making it made me sad too.

# Chapter 13

## *Frank and Margie Olive*

On July 8, 1973, I went to Camp Easter Seal for my fifth year, this time near Waco, Georgia . There I met a young man who was a counselor. He was Frank M. Olive from Augusta, Georgia, and a sophomore at Mercer University. Frank's girlfriend was working there also as a counselor.

The first words Frank said to me were, "Let's start business."

In my cabin were Frank and one other counselor and five campers and me.

That night we had a campfire to meet everybody. Frank took me over to introduce me to his girlfriend Margie O. Gould. To my surprise, this girl who got around so well was blind.

One day at camp I was in the lunch line. Frank got in front of me and suddenly my crutch was going up in the air. Guess where it landed—on Frank's forehead!

The camp "Doc" saw Frank on the ground and asked, "Is the crutch all right?"

It was about two months later when Frank and I met again. I had invited Frank and Margie over to my house for supper one Friday night. After we ate, Frank told tales about some of the jobs he had had. Once he had worked in a funeral home in Augusta. I was surprised to learn that a funeral home is supposed to have someone on guard twenty-four hours a day.

About four months later I started seeing Frank almost every Saturday. We went to movies, to ball games, out to eat, to Mercer University, or to just ride around. One day, while my father was running for the Board of Education, we went to drug stores in the Macon area to put out his campaign posters. In spite of Margie's handicap, being born blind, she excelled in college. Both she and Frank graduated from Mercer University in Macon.

In December 1974 Frank and Margie got married in Augusta. The wedding was on a rainy Saturday. My mother and I drove to the wedding and the reception. As I was coming out of the church's fellowship hall, I saw Paul (Frank's roommate at Mercer) putting some white cream and blue paper all over Frank's car. As my mother and I were driving along the road coming home we saw lots of blue paper on the highway and knew they had lost it. They went to Charleston, South Carolina, on their honeymoon.

In July 1975 Frank and Margie moved back to their home town, Augusta, for awhile. Frank hoped to get a job with a drug company in the Southeast.

In March 1976 I went to Augusta to see Frank and Margie. I went on the bus and Frank met me. They were fine, both working with government jobs. This was a fun visit. Frank and I did many things. We put a CB in his new car, drove all around Augusta, and went to a movie at eleven at night.

Today, after being married several years, Frank and Margie are divorced.

# Chapter 14

## *Early Attempts to Get a Better Education*

I continued to go to the T. D. Tinsley School of Special Education and to enjoy if for many years. As it was the only school I had ever been to, I had no appreciation of what I was getting or not getting academically. However, after I had been in Mrs. Exie Williams's class, the upper special education class, for several years, it became apparent to my parents that I was doing the same lessons over and over, year after year. This lack of advancement was very distressing to them. So they kept putting pressure on the principal, teachers, and other school authorities to give me more challenging work. My parents even wanted me to try some regular courses. A state law had been passed that handicapped children had to be "mainstreamed" as much as possible.

But Bibb County public school officials seemed to pay little attention to this law. And the head of elementary special education for the county—the new lady who succeeded Mrs. Poythress—constantly insisted there was no way I could ever pass even one course in any subject outside of Special Education.

My parents, especially my father, kept asking Mrs. Williams if she could not give me some more advanced work. Apparently she could not, as the Bibb County school system seemed to hold her to teaching only from the simple textbooks prescribed.

Since it became more and more evident that no higher level teaching material could be obtained in this class, my parents became obsessed with the idea that I should be given the opportunity to take at least some schoolwork in a regular class or school. I did not know then, but know now, that my parents became greatly worried about this situation, especially during the 1972–1973 school year, and intensively sought to do something about it.

When I entered Mrs. Williams's class in September 1972 I was thirteen—almost fourteen—years old, and this would be my sixth year in her class and my tenth year at Tinsley. I was getting up in teenage years, it was obvious that I could not stay in this school much longer, and I was getting badly behind academically.

In the fall of 1972 my parents repeatedly talked to Mrs. Williams and to the principal Mrs Molleson about my situation. Toward the end of getting a complete evaluation of my abilities, my folks took me to a prestigious group of Ph.D. psychologists in Atlanta, headed by Dr. R. Wayne Jones. The first time I went, in November 1972, I was evaluated and tested for many hours by Dr. Emil S. Karp, also a Ph.D. Then I went back again in early December, and was tested and evaluated nearly all day by Dr. Jones himself. These doctors' practices were limited exclusively to giving extensive "psychoeducational evaluations" of children.

Dr. Jones sent his many-page exhaustive report to my school that same month. In it Dr. Jones said I had at least normal intelligence, and he felt I should be given the chance to try some regular school work. He had also promised to phone Mrs. Molleson, the principal, and talk to her in more detail about me and about what their tests had shown. Even with his report, in their hands, the Tinsley authorities said they could take no action until Dr. Jones phoned.

The response at my school was typical.

The principal said to my parents, "Why did you take Gary to psychologists in Atlanta? If we had known you *wanted* Gary to be checked by a psychologist, we would have sent him to one of the psychology consultants for the Bibb County school system!"

This, of course, completely missed the point of why we had done it.

Dr. Jones finally called Mrs. Molleson on February 14, 1973, and told her again that I should take some regular classes. But nothing changed. For the remainder of that school year I continued to do the same lessons.

Dr. Jones had also recommended that I take remedial reading, and I started taking it in January or February of 1973, and took it for years.

# Chapter 15

## *Finally Getting "Mainstreamed"*

In September 1973 I started back in Mrs. Exie Williams's class again, my seventh year in her class and my eleventh year in the special education section at T. D. Tinsley. I was fourteen. Even though a few students stayed in Mrs. Williams's class to an older age, it was strongly felt that this would probably be my last year there. What would happen to me at the end of this school year? And was there any way I could take harder courses during this year?

These problems greatly concerned my father and mother, so that fall they kept begging the school to let me try some harder classes. My parents had yet another conference with the principal, Mrs. Molleson, on November 7, 1973. No definitive action came out of this meeting, except plans were made to convene a larger conference in about a week.

In mid-November a very large conference about me was held at the school. Those present were my parents, Mrs. Molleson, the curriculum development lady and reading instructor for many schools, a math teacher from Tinsley regular school, the head lady of elementary special education for Bibb County, and several others. (The special education head was the same lady who had previously vetoed my taking any regular courses.)

In this meeting it was brought out that a new system of modern math, which was already in some Bibb schools, was shortly coming to Tinsley. This math was developed by the educational division of the Xerox Corporation, and was called IMS, for Individualized Mathematics System. It was part of a larger Xerox package called IGE (Individualized Guided Education.) The IMS was to become part of the curriculum at Tinsley after Christmas, and was to be offered one period a day in the regular division of the school. Students would work at their own speed. The people present agreed that I should be allowed to take a math test, and if I could pass it, I would be given a trial in an IMS class when it started.

I took the test in December 1973 and passed it without any trouble. But the IMS math did not start right after Christmas; it started in mid-February 1974. I was thrilled to finally be allowed to go down the forbidden hallway to the regular main part of Tinsley to take this math one period a day, alongside regular, nonhandicapped pupils.

All the writing was done on special Xerox plastic slates which could only be written on by special pencils. After successfully answering the math problems the slate would be wiped clean, and the pupil could go on to the next lesson and a new slate, as fast as he was able.

At the start of this, I was only able to do math at about the second grade level. It was important that I advance as rapidly as possible. Just before I started this course my father called the head of the Xerox educational programs. This man was very sympathetic, because, after Daddy told him about me, he said he had had a cerebral palsied roommate in his college days, whom he had admired greatly. The Xerox man said he would be glad to sell my father the whole system, although before this Xerox had never sold the system to an individual, only to schools and school systems. He shipped it priority shipping, and we got it the next day, about my second day in the class.

In IMS, the student could go at his own speed. Since I had the system at home, every night I would practice the next day's lessons. Then the next day in class I would go like wildfire! We did not feel at all that this was cheating, as the whole intent of this math system is for the student to go through it as rapidly as he can, just so he learns it. I have always had good "number sense," and I did learn it. And, of course, I needed to catch up because of being so far behind.

Although school did not end until about June first, for some unknown reason all the IMS math at Tinsley was stopped in mid-April. But in those *two months*, working less than an hour five days a week, I had gone through *four or five grades* of math!

When the IMS ended, my father was so fearful that I could not get a good education in Macon or in Georgia that, on the recommendation of my remedial reading instructor and former next-door neighbor Fil Campbell (now Mullis), he called Mike Weinroth, chief of special education for the State of Georgia, and asked him about me. Mr. Weinroth told my father that, in view of the strong Georgia law saying that the state was required to provide the best education possible for the handicapped, he would approve state funds to send me to any school in the United States my parents wanted me to attend. However, he urged my father to try hard to get me better education locally before going to these lengths, and to wait and see where the Bibb authorities would send me the next school year. He did send forms to complete to apply for this aid from the state, but we never filled them out.

Sure enough, at the end of that 1973–1974 school year, I was advised that I could not go back to Tinsley, but should go to Miller A, a junior high school, for assignment in September.

In July 1974 my father showed up on the 6:00 p.m. local TV news with the story that he was running for an elected seat on the Bibb County Board of Education. My brother Clark was the first to hear this TV report, and he screamed for all of us to come and watch. This was a great shock to the whole family, as Daddy had not told any of us he was entering politics, not even Mother! But, after a little bit, we became accustomed to the idea, and we all worked hard on his campaign.

I went to Easter Seal camp again that summer, in 1974. This was my last of six straight years of summer Easter Seal camps, four years in Georgia camps (Magnolia Springs, Waco, and Fort Yargo twice,) and the last two years at Camp Easter-N-the-Pines in North Carolina. I could not enjoy the camp much because I was worried about school. I knew that in about two months I was going to Miller A, but did not know into what kind of class or classes.

When I reported to Miller A in late August I was shocked and disappointed to find I had been put in a class in the eighth grade with mentally retarded students. The work was childish, and I would only be allowed to stay at school until 11:45 a.m.! There was no way I could get any significant education in this setting.

My parents, of course, were greatly distressed that I was now taking schoolwork much simpler than I had been getting at Tinsley, and that I would not even be allowed to stay until lunch time. In a few weeks I was changed from the mentally retarded class at Miller A to a mentally retarded class at Miller B High School. But nothing had really changed.

In October my mother begged one of the head ladies at Miller B to allow me to stay a little later—at least through lunch—and that I be allowed to go to a higher level class. But she refused to do anything, and no changes were made. But Mother would not let things stand like that. She decided she needed a conference with the principal of Miller B, whom she had known most of her life, and who she felt was a friend. So she asked for a private audience with him, to talk about my situation, and a date was set for early November.

But when Mother got to his office at the appointed time, she was surprised to find not only the principal, but a whole lot of other people, teachers and administrators! Then they all attacked her and scolded her for calling this "meeting" and asked her what was she trying to do, and why was she bothering them? Mother tried to tell them that I was going nowhere, that I had normal intelligence, and should not be in a class with the mentally retarded. She tried to explain that she had called for no meeting, but had only intended to have a private conference with the principal. Mother asked them why I could not stay in school until 3:00 p.m. like everyone else, and she begged them to mainstream me, as the law required.

At this they all became angry and acted very ugly to Mother. They said they were already doing more for me than anyone had a right to expect, that we should be grateful, and they made a lot of other rude remarks. They fussed at Mother, told her to leave them alone, not to ask for anything else, and they were not going to change anything.

Mother came home and was so depressed that she cried for three days, although at that time I did not know why. She told me about this meeting much later.

Then, at about that same time, in spite of a long, hard, and expensive campaign in which the whole family had participated deeply, my father narrowly lost the school board election. But the next day the superintendent of the Bibb County Board of Education, Dr. Thomas Lott, wrote Daddy a thank you letter for running a good clean race, and stated that if my father ever needed anything just to let him know. On the basis of that, Daddy called Dr. Lott and made an appointment with him for eleven the next morning (but did not say what he wanted to talk about).

At that meeting my father discussed my situation with Dr. Lott, explaining that I was sixteen, but was being given only first- or second-grade-level work. Daddy had taken some of my ridiculously easy papers, on which I had made A's, and showed them to the superintendent. Dr. Lott was very interested and concerned, and agreed with father that Gary Mann should have a chance to get a regular education.

Dr. Lott started the ball rolling, to see that something would be done. He assigned Ms. Ann Henry, his curriculum coordinator, to proceed on this task at once. She was instructed to find the best place for me, in a regular school, and not in Special Education. Ms. Henry immediately took on the task of looking for a good spot in the system for me.

In a day or two, while Ms. Henry was searching, word from on high must have gotten down to the authorities at Miller B, as they started letting me walk up and down stairs, eat in the lunchroom with someone carrying my tray, and stay at school until 1:00 p.m.—things Mother had just begged for which they said they could not allow. While I climbed stairs or went through the lunch line, assigned faculty members secretly spied on me, to see how I did! I think they must have been upset when I did not fall on my face, as in the conference with Mother they had said such activities would be impossible for me to accomplish.

Ms. Henry reported to Dr. Lott that she thought she had found just the right spot in *regular education* for me. She thought I should transfer to a regular school, Ballard B Junior High School, in the eighth grade. Ballard B is part of the Southwest complex. At that time Southwest was one of the largest high schools in the entire United States, with about 3,500 students, and it was one of the toughest. This proposal was subject to the approval of Dr. Lott and the Ballard instructors.

I went to Ballard B, took a good many tests to evaluate my learning to that point, and was interviewed by the principal, Dr. Ludlam, and by several teachers. They seemed to be satisfied that I would fit in and could do eighth-grade work.

So December 2 was my last day at Miller B in the mentally retarded class. On December 3, 1974, I finally achieved my long-held dream, to be allowed to go all day to a regular public school! Now it would be just up to me to study hard and pass. I did not worry that the students might not accept me, as I knew they would.

I was very proud to be the first multihandicapped student ever to be fully mainstreamed in Bibb County, Georgia.

## Chapter 16

# *Adjusting to Regular Education*

From the first day, I enjoyed being in school in the eighth grade at Ballard B. The class I was put in was not in special education. The program I began on December 3, 1974, had classrooms in "clusters." This program had been developed to keep students in the same group of classrooms or clusters all day. For example, I would be in a classroom with a group for social studies, then the entire class would move through a door in the wall to another room to study another subject. There were about twenty-five pupils doing schoolwork at their own speed. All of us would spend fifty minutes in one class, and then go next door. We were on the semester system. All the students were friendly, and I seemed to be doing all right with my schoolwork. But *none* of the teachers had ever had anything to do with a handicapped person, and they were puzzled by me and afraid of me.

So, on December 17, 1974, only two weeks after I had been there, the Ballard B teachers and authorities had a called meeting with my parents. The faculty members said they liked me, but every one of them said bad things about me. They complained that they had never been trained or asked before to teach someone like me, that my handwriting was too hard to read, they could not understand my speech, assigning a student to carry my tray at lunch was a lot of trouble, students would make fun of me and knock me down in the halls (this never happened), and so forth. They further stated that there was no way I could walk between the staggered tables in the cluster classroom because the table corners were close together, and I used a crutch. (I had been walking between the tables for two weeks with no problem.) And why did I just use one crutch? They had heard of one using two crutches, but never one. My folks tried to explain that I had formerly used two crutches, but had progressed to needing only one.

The teachers gave lots more stupid "reasons" why I should not be imposed on them. But, fortunately, my good friend and proponent Ms. Ann Henry was there, representing the school board. Ms. Henry stated she thought all I needed was a little help, and toward this end she would assign a special education teacher to me one period a day, during study hall, just to go over my regular subject lessons, and to help me where needed. At this, the teachers all relaxed, and said they would be glad to try this for awhile. Then all of my teachers even started saying good things about me!

So I stayed in that eighth grade class, and then the Christmas holidays came along. In January 1975 the faculty had another conference with my parents. This time they told the totally opposite story, now saying I was doing fine at Ballard B, and they had all known all along that I could manage in regular school okay! I wondered if *all* my teachers had thought this, and, if so, why had not they been more supportive of my parents and me all those years before when I had been trying so hard to change from special to regular education?

On January 25, 1975, I got my first rcport card ever in regular school, for the first semester of the eighth grade. I received an A, a B, and two C's.

The second semester at Ballard B I had some new teachers and some new subjects, but everything went smoothly, and I made good grades and had no trouble passing. The special education lady continued to work with me one period a day, and she really helped me in my first year in regular school. I also was allowed to bring my electric typewriter to school. I kept it on a rolling stand no bigger than the typewriter, so I could move it from class to class. Now no one had any trouble reading my reports. This semester I made A's and B's.

During the summer vacation following the eighth grade I changed from using one crutch to one cane, to walk anywhere, even outside; and I continued writing on this book, which I had started the year before at age fifteen.

In the fall of 1975 I started back at Ballard B Junior High School for the ninth grade, but things were very different this year. Bibb County schools had been on the semester system for fifty to one hundred years. But, beginning that September, for the first time ever, suddenly all schools were put on the quarter system. And this year I no longer had any special situation—I was not in a clustered classroom, and had no special education lady helping me. I was treated no differently from any other student. It was surely good that I had been there the year before, but even so, it was hard to get used to this new system. In fact, many of the students had trouble adjusting to the quarter system: having been familiar with long semesters, some of the students let midterm and final examinations slip up on them and they flunked out. However, I continued to do well, with almost all my grades being A's and B's.

In Macon at that time all the junior high schools were for the eighth and ninth grades; and the senior high schools were for the tenth, eleventh, and twelfth grades. I was doing so well in the ninth grade at Ballard B, and they liked me so much, that they started putting pressure on me to take my senior high school classes there, beginning the next year. But I was determined instead, for the tenth grade, to go to Central (Lanier) High School, whose school district I was in, and to which most of my friends went.

## Chapter 17

# *Pneumonia—Not a Simple Sickness*

For the spring holidays of 1976 I went to my cousin's cottage in Fernandina Beach, Florida, for five days. My sister Beverly and my brothers David and Clark came down to join us.

The night before we were supposed to leave the beach to come home, my side started hurting, so my doctor father looked me over and said, "I think it is where you held the fishing pole against your body yesterday."

A day later we came back to Macon, but my side was still hurting.

I went back to school the next day and was all right. But that afternoon my side started hurting again, but not as bad. So I went to choir practice and was supposed to go to Scout meeting after that. But about fifteen minutes before choir practice the pain got really bad.

So my mother came and got me and took me to my father's office. The next day I went to get X rays from Dr. Cato and he said that I had pleurisy. My father put me on some drugs and hoped I would be all right soon.

A few days passed, but I was no better, so my father talked to another doctor, and he said for me to be admitted to the Coliseum Park Hospital. So I entered the hospital. They took blood tests. That night they started an IV going and it stayed for ten days. The next day I got X-rayed again and they said that I had pneumonia as well as pleurisy, plus fluid around my lung. During this long hospital stay I had needles stuck into my chest fourteen times to drain this fluid. That was most unpleasant!

While in the hospital I had many visitors from my youth group. It was a nice that two of my teachers from Ballard B brought my yearbook to me.

By now I was getting worried if I would be strong enough to go to the performance of the youth musical *Love*, that I had worked on for four months with my choir. But I was too weak to go, so my father taped it for me. I was discharged from the hospital on Easter Sunday.

Another big thing happened that Easter Sunday. Riverside broke ground for a new sanctuary. My grandfather, Rev. David Mann, who had founded this church, was to do the groundbreaking. Arrangements had been made with the church ahead of time so that, if I got dismissed from the hospital in time to get to this service, we would be allowed to drive up across the church grounds to the spot where the groundbreaking would be held. My brother Clark held a space open between two parked cars, to make a driveway opening to the site. I was fortunate to get discharged from the hospital just in time to get to the ceremony. My grandfather handed me the very first shovelful of dirt he dug up: he brought it over to the car where I was sitting, so I could save it as a remembrance of the occasion.

When I went back to the choir they gave me a Bible because I had been sick and had missed singing with them in the musical *Love.*

## Chapter 18

# *Big Apple, Tall Ships*

On July 1, 1976, my father, my mother, and I went to the Atlanta airport. It was a good day for flying. The flight was smooth and we went up to 33,000 feet. It was flight 116 on a Delta jet. They served a full lunch on the plane, which was delicious.

When we got to the Newark, New Jersey, airport we had to wait for the bus to take us to Manhattan. We checked into the Taft Hotel, but this hotel was not the type for us because it was very run-down. So we got a room at the nearest Howard Johnson's. When we got settled in the motel in mid-Manhattan, we got a fast supper there.

The next day my father called some publishers about this book, and we went to several of them on Madison Avenue. We were surprised how easy it was to actually get in and talk to the presidents of several large publishing houses! They were all nice to us, but said they thought this autobiographical story was unfinished in its form then—which was true. Some of the publishers said they did not publish this type of book.

When we got back to the motel I read some more of *Why Not the Best?* by Jimmy Carter, of whom I was a big fan then.

This was all during the nation's bicentennial celebration, and there were big crowds everywhere. That evening we took a cab to the McGraw-Hill building to see "New York Experience."

Saturday morning we went to the top of the Empire State Building. The view was breathtaking. For souvenirs, I bought a small model of the building, as well as some playing cards with a picture of it on them.

That afternoon we went to see the Broadway play *Shenandoah*, starring John Cullum, and it was great. While there I met a man from

Savannah, Georgia. My mother met one of the boys who was in the play and got his autograph. That night we went to see the Rockettes and a sorry movie at Radio City Music Hall, but the Rockettes were great! After the show we got caught in a huge parade on Fifth Avenue. It was like New Year's Eve on Time's Square.

On the nation's two hundredth birthday we went to Battery Park on the southern end of Manhattan. There were more than six million people in the crowd. In Battery Park we soon discovered there was no way we would be able to see the ships. So we moved north by cab up the Hudson River, and we found a very good view. It was exciting watching all the beautiful tall sailing ships go by. That night we went to the lobbies of the newest hotels in Manhattan, the Americana and the New York Hilton hotels. After that we called it a day.

The next day we went on a six-hour Gray Line tour of lower and upper New York, plus the Statue of Liberty. Just a few places we saw were Chinatown, the World Trade Center, the United Nations building, Rockefeller Center, Central Park, and Columbia University. We toured St. John's Cathedral. It is the second largest church building in the world. We also saw the sometime homes of Johnny Carson, Jackie Kennedy Onassis, Katherine Hepburn, Joan Crawford, and of other noted people.

The next day was the last and the most important day for us in New York—and the reason we went there. On this day I had an appointment to see the famous neurosurgeon Dr. Irving S. Cooper. He was very late for the appointment, but we finally met, he examined me, and we got along well. I liked him very much. I found out that first he got his Ph.D., then later his M.D.

Dr. Cooper had been around the world at least four times, and he also spoke six languages. He was the author of six books, and he gave me a copy of one of his books, and I gave him a copy of this book. It was an even deal.

Dr. Cooper had invented an operation for people who have cerebral palsy and other diseases. In the operation he would put a pacemaker in the brain, and he suggested it for me. Before surgery I would have to be in the hospital fourteen days and have tests, to be sure the operation would help me. I wanted the operation, but if I had it this summer, I would have to miss the Fall quarter of school. Dr. Cooper said it would be all right for me to wait and get it the next summer, and to contact his office in early 1977. That is what we decided to do.

It was a very nice trip to New York. We flew back that same night, getting home about 2:00 a.m.

## Chapter 19

# *A Wonderful Youth Choir Tour*

After hours and days of practicing, we were ready to go on our long-planned tour. So Buddy Johstono, the choir director, rented an extra van. It was a cargo van. With the church van (really a small bus) we already had, that was enough.

Our first concert was on Sunday at our home church, Riverside, where we sang just a few of our songs. That night we gave the first complete rendition of our musical concert *Love* at Perry, a town about thirty miles from Macon. A host of Riverside members came to listen.

Monday morning we headed north. Craig and Doug Pyles, former Maconites, had come down from Charlotte, their new home, to join the tour. In Atlanta we stopped for lunch at a restaurant in Underground Atlanta. After the meal we walked around that tourist area.

Then we went to Doraville, Georgia, to the Kingswood United Methodist Church. We found it to be a church surrounded by trees, similar to our Riverside church. We went inside, set up, and ran through some of our music.

That Monday night we gave our concert at this church. After the performance everyone went to private homes to spend the night. Cary Stinnett and I stayed with a nice family. Because I had forgotten my toothbrush, they gave me a new one.

The next morning, Tuesday, we got up and dressed, and were pleased to find that our hostess had fixed us a big and delicious breakfast. After eating, they took Cary and me back to the church, and everybody told about his and her experiences, and the people each had met.

Soon we were in the bus and riding again. On the way to our next stop we went through the town of Dahlonega, Georgia, and having a little spare time, we visited the Dahlonega Gold Museum. Then we went to a local restaurant and had a great country lunch, with many meats and vegetables. Then we went to Gainesville, Georgia, a small city, to St. Paul's United Methodist Church, where we started getting ready for our concert.

Our performance that night of our musical *Love* seemed unusually good, as the acoustics in this sanctuary were great.

There were thirty-one youth members on the tour. In addition there were some older people who were counselors.

After the concert that night we slept in the church building. About 3:00 or 4:00 a.m. a policeman noticed that a door was unlocked, so he came in and searched the place. He found us, thought we looked suspicious, and seemed to think a crime was taking place. But finally Don Clarke and one of the mothers were able to convince the policeman that we were a Christian group and not a bunch of robbers!

After that unsettling night, the next morning Buddy suddenly decided that we needed to take some exercise. He made the youth do push-ups, sit-ups, running assignments, and other exercises. He excused me from these activities, so I just stayed in the van and watched them sweat.

Then we got in the van and traveled to Bryson City, North Carolina. Many of us went down Deep Creek in inner tubes. That was a lot of fun. Too bad that Buddy lost his glasses in the water and had to wear two pair, one on top of the other, in order to see. That made him look really funny. After we finished playing with the inner tubes, some of the others and I stayed in the creek and took a bath in the cold water.

After this recreation at the creek near Bryson City, Don talked to one of the rangers about our putting on our presentation of *Love* at a campsite there. The ranger said all right, so we started setting up our equipment. But, unfortunately, a piece of the tape player was missing. We looked on the ground for it for more than twenty minutes, but it was nowhere to be found. We could not sing without the tape, because it contained all the instrumental music and sound efforts. So we had to leave the campsite, telling the people that we were sorry we were unable to give the program. To make things worse, as we were driving off, many more people were just coming to hear us.

In Bryson City proper we went out for a late supper. Most of us got seafood. I love fried shrimp so much, I had no problem deciding to order it from the menu. The church gave us all three dollars toward this meal, but, not surprisingly, mine cost more, so I paid the difference.

We spent that Wednesday night in Bryson City, but the next morning we drove to Cherokee, North Carolina, for breakfast. Cherokee is full of Indians. Most of us had never seen a real Indian before. For breakfast I only ordered a carton of milk and two huge doughnuts, but that filled me up.

Then we went by Lake Junaluska, North Carolina, a retreat owned by the Methodist church for people in the Southeast to use. We rested at the big cross beside the lake. This was very peaceful. Later we drove by the hotel there and the Methodist conference center.

Then we went on to Charlotte, to St. Stephens United Methodist Church. This was Craig's and Doug's new church. This church also resembled our own Riverside church, but not as much as Kingswood had.

Before the concert Don called for all of us to make a prayer circle. This was not unusual, because we had a prayer circle every night. But this one was the most meaningful, because no one was in the right mood to give our program.

So Don said, "Step in the circle if you are ready to serve God."

Everybody stepped in.

And we did fine in the concert.

After the service we all went over to Craig's and Doug's new home for a time of fellowship. I met some nice Charlotte young people. I talked to a young girl there who was interested in this book. She asked me why I named my book "Living in Georgia with Cerebral Palsy," the tentative title of my book at that time.

I said, "I live in Georgia and I have cerebral palsy."

Then we sang until 11:30 p.m. After that we went back to the church and spent the night. Doug and Craig left their home and spent the night with us in the church also.

Friday was the last day of the tour. First we took Doug and Craig home, then got on the road back to Georgia right after breakfast.

The tour was very nice and I enjoyed every minute of it. We had sung to more than 600 people (not including those at Riverside) and had gone about 900 miles. We got home about 5:30 p.m., tired and dirty, but happy.

Chapter 20

# *The Big Orange*

After finishing the ninth grade at Ballard B Junior High School of the Southwest complex, for the tenth grade I was advanced to Lanier B Senior High School of the Central complex. This school was better known by its nickname, the "Big Orange."

On that first day of the fall quarter, on August 30, 1976, I entered this big building. I saw lots of students mixed up about where to go.

I thought, "Is the Big Orange too big for me?" (although it was not as big as Ballard) and "How am I going to like Lanier B?"

Though I had been in this school a few days before to register, and even once or twice before that as a visitor, I suddenly realized I was no longer a guest but a student.

Central is one of the finest schools in the Southeast. In fact, it is the high school my father graduated from. He graduated the same year as the school principal, Mr. Elton Wall. My two brothers, several former teachers, and some of my older friends had also gone there.

The old Lanier B building burned down in 1967. And now standing on the same site is a beautiful new building, with orange and white walls in the halls, and black beams dividing the classrooms. Also there are orange lockers in the halls.

The Big Orange is made up of four buildings: Miller A and Miller B for eighth and ninth grade students; and Lanier A and Lanier B for senior (tenth through twelfth grade) high school boys and girls. Lanier A was for the girls' supervision classes and Lanier B was for the boys' supervision classes when I was a student. However, now Lanier A and B classes are mostly coed. My mother knew a Social Studies teacher there, Mrs. Bettye Parker, and she was a big help to me in my introduction to Lanier B. She paved the way by helping me select the best courses and the most understanding teachers for me. Later I took American History from her. All of the students liked Mrs. Parker; she was one of the most popular teachers there.

Almost every Friday during football season we would have a pep rally. We would do cheers and sing. These rallies were held on the football practice field.

The next-to-last football game of the season featured Central versus Southwest, who are bitter rivals. The game was boring until the last quarter, when both teams scored. But Southwest missed the point after its touchdown, and Central won the game 7–6. I was there and joined in the excitement of the victory!

My first quarter at Lanier B I took Biology, Grammar, Government, and Algebra, and I worked in the library. The librarian was Mrs. Frances Harrison. She and I made a deal that when it was raining she would let me put my raincoat in the library all day, and when this book is published I will give her a free copy. Mrs. Harrison was a fast talker, and would talk almost the whole time I was in the library.

Every day I would leave Mrs. Harrison to go to my next class with Professor Johnson. As I would enter his room, Professor Johnson would always ask me, "Has Mrs. Harrison been talking much today?"

My Biology teacher was Mrs. Campbell. She was a good teacher, but I did not make really good grades because I made some careless mistakes.

My Grammar teacher was Mrs. Booker and she was a tough instructor, but I learned to like her. Since I am a bad speller and Mrs. Booker watched for spelling, at least she helped me learn to spell better.

My Algebra teacher was Mr. John Swint. Mr. Swint believed in homework every night, and in doing every problem in the textbook. Since I am a slow writer, he and I made a deal so I only worked every other problem for homework. This algebra was complicated and hard, but I was able to make good grades in it.

My homeroom teacher was a full-blooded Creek Indian named Mr. Gerald Harjo. He had been born and raised in Oklahoma. His brother was in the first Billy Jack movie.

I carried a brown briefcase to school every day. Since my briefcase had a limited amount of space, the school let me have two sets of books in each subject, one for home and one for the classroom.

Those first three months at Central many years ago brought me happiness. I became part of the "Big Orange"!

## Chapter 21

# *Garo and the Peanut*

Going back to August 30, 1976, my first day at the "Big Orange," I did not know whether to be carefree or serious. At fourth period that day I walked into room 301 and found a funny, gray-haired professor. His name was Gus Johnson.

That first quarter Mr. Johnson taught a course about politics. Little did I know that would be a journey through my funniest class ever. He was a comical, crazy, wild, bald-headed Baptist, and a *peanut.*

The reason I nicknamed him Peanut was because he was a big fan of Jimmy Carter's, and he was raised about twenty miles from Plains, Carter's home, but he had never met the presidential candidate.

Peanut would steal jokes from Johnny Carson and tell them to the class the next day.

One of his jokes was: "Do you know why President Ford fired Henry Kissinger?"

"Because he found some peanuts in his pocket."

Another was: "Do you know who waked the Ford's up at 3:00 a.m. the night of the election?"

"It was Rosalyn Carter measuring the windows for drapes!"

In Mr. Johnson's class we would discuss the presidential campaign. Some student would give a newspaper report every day on each candidate's progress. In addition to that, we would have to keep up with what was going on by reading magazine reports, listening to the radio, watching TV, and by using other materials. Peanut told us to watch a special on the campaign, "Battle for the White House," on ABC. I watched it, but Peanut went to a football game instead!

He loved to show films, and Peanut would show a film two or three times a week. I think he was a little unfair to me, because he would always start showing them about twenty minutes before the period was over. Since I had to leave class five minutes early in order to get to my next class on time, I missed the endings of some good films. But I did see a few of them completely.

At lunch Peanut and I would try to steal each other's food. He would try to steal my apple pie and I would try to swipe his sandwich and milk. He sat by me most of the time, and when he would get some napkins with his back turned, I would put his milk and sandwich in my lap.

After lunch we would go to his room and he would get his box of vanilla wafers out, and he would always give me one. Then we would talk a little bit, usually about girls, Riverside United Methodist Church, Vineville Baptist Church (Peanut's church), and a few other topics. We would stand in the hall until fifth period and watch the people go by. A few times he made me late for my next class in Biology.

When fifth period was over during the second quarter, I usually stopped by his room and got my Economics book—I took Economics from Peanut that quarter—to finish my work in it that day in the library. One day I was bringing his book back and he tried to assault me with a broom, for interrupting his class, but he was playing, as usual.

Peanut thought everybody should own a few shares of stock. He got upset when his stocks were down, and happy when they were high. The first thing he did when he got home every day was to study the stock market for an hour—or two or three.

Since leaving Lanier I have talked to Peanut a few times on the phone. I invited him to come to Riverside Church to hear my choir do *Alleluia*. He came and enjoyed it very much.

My letter from the ex-mayor was the subject of our second phone discussion. I had written my neighbor and former Macon Mayor Buck Melton about having a school holiday on the presidential inauguration day, since Jimmy Carter was the former governor of Georgia. Melton's answer in the letter was "Maybe." But a fuel shortage developed and extremely cold weather closed the schools. So we all got a holiday and got to watch the inauguration on TV anyway.

My last discussion with Peanut was my April Fools' joke: I told him I was moving to New York the next day.

Before I finished talking Peanut asked, "Is this an April Fools' joke?"

I replied, "Yes," laughing then, but I had managed to stay serious as I was saying it.

All in all, I think Gus Peanut Johnson was about the funniest fellow I ever worked with.

He is retired now, but I see him occasionally.

Chapter 22

# *Booted Out of the Boy Scouts*

When I was about fourteen years old my parents found out about a Boy Scout troop for the handicapped in Macon, Troop 209. I joined this troop, which was sponsored by the Disabled American Veterans, with three or four other handicapped boys. Troop 209 was geared to serve the handicapped of many types, including the mentally and emotionally impaired. Several veterans dedicated their time to help this small troop, which never had more than about six members.

We met once a week in the D.A.V. building. We would go camping about twice a year, and this was a lot of fun. I seemed to be the only one there interested in advancing in rank in the Boy Scouts. Our main project was to take a bicycle apart. This took the troop several months. Then we would put the bicycle back together again. Other than this, the troop did nothing special. After about two years, I got tired of going to this troop and doing the same things, although the scoutmaster and other veterans running the troop were very kind, and they were concerned with what they thought was best for us.

We called the scoutmaster of regular Boy Scout Troop 8, based at my church, Riverside United Methodist, to see if maybe I could transfer to it. It met every week at the scout hut on the church grounds. This was an unusual request in the Boy Scouts, because handicapped boys were always put in troops numbered 200 or higher, as I was. The Troop 8 Scoutmaster said for me to visit his troop at its regular Wednesday night meetings for a trial period, to see if the boys would accept me, and to see if they thought I could make it in a regular troop. So I started visiting, and in a few weeks Troop 8 accepted me as a regular member.

Troop 8 was better organized than Troop 209. Here the leaders really helped the Scouts advance and earn Merit Badges, which I started doing right away. In Troop 209 I had reached Tenderfoot and Second Class Scout levels.

I was proud to be in this new troop, worked hard, and advanced rapidly. Merit Badges and other awards were given out once a month at special ceremonies called Courts of Honor, and parents were invited. After six months, at a Troop 8 Court of Honor I was awarded the First Class Boy Scout rating and six Merit Badges—Auto Safety, First Aid, Photography, Public Health, Safety, and Stamp Collecting. This was great, as I was the only handicapped boy in the troop, but received more merit badges than any other member. I was very proud to be so honored.

I continued working hard. Being in this troop was a highlight of my life to that time. I attained the Star Scout level, which requires five Merit Badges plus some other specifications. The only two higher levels in Scouts than Star are Life Scout and Eagle Scout. The main requirement for Life Scout is to get ten merit badges, some of which are required; and to attain Eagle Scout one must earn twenty-one merit badges, many of which are required. Of course, I wanted to go "all the way."

I had been in Troop 8 for less than two years, and was still progressing rapidly, when all my hopes were dashed by a "bombshell" that was dropped on me.

In early October 1976 the scoutmaster of Troop 8 contacted me and said, "Gary, I notice that on October 9 you will be eighteen years old. The Boy Scouts of America does not let anyone remain in the Scouts after his eighteenth birthday, so you will have to get out then."

That was only six days away! The scoutmaster said that was the rule, but we had had no knowledge whatsoever of it before now. I felt this was unfair, as I was doing so well. I also thought some consideration should be given to the fact that I had been delayed on advancement for years by being in that handicapped troop.

My father pleaded with the scoutmaster and with others, including my minister friend and pastor of the church where the troop is located. He went to see the head of the Central Georgia Boy Scout Council, which is located in Macon. All of these leaders said they knew no way to change the situation.

Failing to get local help, my father called and talked a long time with the associate director of the Boy Scouts of America, in New Brunswick, New Jersey. This man said he could do nothing, and he did not seem especially interested. Daddy called him back the next day, again trying to explain my unusual circumstances and asking if some waiver or exception might be made in my case. But he remained unchanging in his attitude, insisting no one could stay in the Scouts after becoming eighteen, except for those mentally retarded.

My dream of becoming an Eagle Scout like my father was destroyed. It was unjust that I had worked so hard, had reached First Class Scout, Star Scout, had now earned thirteen merit badges, had partially completed two more, and was almost a Life Scout—only to be kicked out with less than a week's notice. So on my eighteenth birthday I had to drop out of Troop 8 and out of the Boy Scouts.

Some years later I read in the newspaper about a Long Island Boy Scout with cerebral palsy who was denied Eagle Scout by another rule. He sued the Boy Scouts of America, won, and became an Eagle Scout, after the court made the BSA modify its rules so they would be reasonable for a handicapped Scout, at least in this one case.

# Chapter 23

## *The Brain Pacemaker*

In July 1976, when I had seen Dr. Irving Cooper, the famous neurosurgeon in New York, he had said that I was a good candidate for the cerebellar stimulator or "Brain Pacemaker" operation and to contact him the first of the year. So in February 1977 my father wrote Dr. Cooper's office and found out that he was out of the country. Two months later his office called to let us know that Dr. Cooper was no longer doing this surgery! This was somewhat of a relief to us, because we were worried about having the operation in New York City. Dr. Cooper wanted to keep me in the hospital several weeks before and after my surgery. Also the hospital was in a bad neighborhood, I would have to miss some of my school term, and it was a long way from Macon.

But we were still interested in this operation for me. Dr. Hugh Smisson, a Macon doctor and friend of my father's, told him about Dr. Marshall B. Allen, Jr., chief of neurosurgery at Eugene Talmadge Memorial Hospital in Augusta, Georgia, who was doing the brain pacemaker surgery on young patients with cerebral palsy. Dr. Smisson has always been interested in my well-being, both as a friend and as one of the leading neurosurgeons in Macon.

My father, my mother, and I drove to Augusta to see Dr. Allen. He was very kind, fully explained the operation, and left the decision whether to have the surgery or not totally up to us. I made up my mind to have it before my parents did.

In Dr. Allen's first case, he operated on a boy from Aiken, South Carolina, who was eighteen years old. The boy was in a wheelchair, and before the operation he could not hold a sandwich or a hamburger without "squeezing it to death." After his surgery he could write, talk, and eat better. He could also hold food without crushing it. Dr. Allen also had performed surgery on another person, my age, from Warner Robins, Georgia. For eighteen days after the surgery she was in the hospital, and she had headaches for two or three months. She was out of school for twelve weeks, and had to go to summer school to make up for lost time. But in spite of all that, she ended up with a good result.

So we agreed upon this surgery, and the date was set for July 1, 1977.

I entered the Eugene Talmadge Memorial Hospital the day after the funeral of my beloved grandfather, Reverend David G. Mann. I was so blue I felt like postponing or cancelling this surgery, but my folks convinced me that PaPa Mann would have wanted me to go ahead and have it. I was in the hospital three days before the surgery, so they could perform lots of tests on me.

It was so hot in my hospital room that the air conditioner could not cool the air enough. Mother had to walk two blocks to Sears to buy a floor fan.

The night before surgery the anesthesiologist came to see me and said, "Everything will be fine in the operating room."

When they rolled me into the anteroom next to the operating room, all I can remember is the nurses and doctors in their white masks and scrub suits looking down at me. I was in a row of eight people waiting to be operated on.

Even though I was asleep, I found out later that I had been strapped in a special chair during the surgery, and they operated on me sitting up. Dr. Allen made a cut in the back of my head to get to my brain. He put four electrodes on top of my cerebellum on each side. In addition, he made a small incision near my collarbone to implant wires, and a round metal plate under the skin of my right upper chest. When hooked up, the battery current would go to the cerebellar electrodes for seven minutes on and seven minutes off. This current was believed to knock out some of the stray brain currents in patients with cerebral palsy, so their muscles would work better.

After the surgery, which took two hours, they put me in the recovery room for about two more hours before they brought me to my room. The next two days I was mostly sleeping. I remember that all of my family came to see me. Also a lot of dear friends came during my three-week hospital stay.

Don and Elaine Clarke spent the fourth of July with me. They brought me a watermelon. We cut it with Dr. Allen and some nurses. It was the best watermelon we ever ate.

There was a boy on my floor who was sixteen years old and who weighed 200 pounds. He came to see me about four times a day and wanted to talk. We tried to play checkers. He fell in love with Jane, a cute nurse, and said they would get married. After about a week of this, he beat up his roommate and cut him with a knife. They decided he was mentally unbalanced and moved him to another ward. I was glad he did not attack me.

Also on my floor was a six-month-old baby girl. "Becky" had been there for two months, after surgery for an open spine she had had since birth. Her mother abandoned her, but all the nurses loved her.

Assisting Dr. Allen during the surgery was a resident physician from Pakistan named Dr. Malik. Another of the doctors in training was a funny young Italian from Venice. Every time I think of him I cannot help laughing. His name was Dr. Berdusco.

Because of his Italian accent it took me several days to understand him. Every morning he came bursting in at 7:00 a.m. Always with him were about six other doctor-students to observe me.

Three mornings after my operation, when he opened the door, Dr. Berdusco said, "Goo m-o-u-r-n-ing Gary, why you look so g-l-o-o-my? Don't you know dis is der foce of July (4th of July)? Be hoppy (happy), let's celebrate!"

Later he warned me, "Don't you go chussing (chasing) dose nurses down de hall."

One thing you could always count on was Dr. Berdusco. He worked twelve hours every day, even holidays and weekends, at Talmadge Memorial Hospital. Dr. Allen said he was the best resident he had ever had on neurosurgery.

On the fifth of July Dr. Allen turned on the pacemaker. Every few days he would change the settings a little bit. I did not feel anything, and could tell no difference right at first. My recovery from the surgery continued without event, and I was discharged from the hospital after about a three-week stay.

When we went back to Augusta for my first check-up, Dr. Berdusco was *off* for three days and Dr. Malik was working for him. I was glad Dr. Berdusco was having a little vacation, for I had thought he was on duty all the time.

During my hospitalization I had enjoyed working with Kathy Marks and Elaine Hines. Kathy was the occupational therapist and Elaine was the physical therapist. After discharge from the hospital I continued occupational and physical therapy (OT and PT for short) in Macon under Theo Fisher for OT and Margaret Podlesny for PT. I received both therapies at Margaret's home twice a week, until she moved out of town about a year later.

After the operation, my talking was faster and my walking was smoother. As time went on many more improvements from the brain pacemaker took place.

In November 1984 one of my advisors at Mercer noticed that I was falling a lot. She was concerned that something might be wrong with my pacemaker.

My father called Dr. Allen, who immediately suspected that the wires running to my brain might be broken. He ordered "stat" (urgent) X rays of my head, neck, and chest; a stat CT scan of my head; a stat EEG (electroencephalogram), and other tests. We had all these tests run on me and sent them to Dr. Allen by Federal Express. Dr. Allen called us and said the wires were indeed broken. Dr. Allen said to turn off the power, as no power was getting to my brain anyway.

I had had the brain pacemaker for seven years, and Dr. Allen said it was really good that the pacemaker had lasted that long. All of his other patients had quit using their pacemakers. Today no neurosurgeons are doing this procedure.

## Chapter 24

# *The "Affair"*

I was lying in a hospital bed on the third floor of the Eugene Talmadge Memorial Hospital in Augusta. After Dr. Marshall Allen connected the battery to my brain pacemaker, I was sent to Occupational Therapy on the second floor.

The young lady who was my occupational therapist was twenty-four years old. I was eighteen years old and was still weak from the pacemaker surgery. So on that first visit I was more interested in recovering than in the opposite sex. But Kathy was so beautiful that I was sorry I had to meet her as a patient.

She was a wonderful therapist and took a personal interest in me. I was just in the tenth grade but I had a crush on her.

I said to myself, "What shall I do with this woman?"

I thought of my first cousin Fred Daniel, a medical student there, who had just broken up with his girlfriend. So I told Kathy about Fred, but she was not interested.

The next fall, when I was went back to Augusta to be rechecked by Dr. Allen, I stopped by the Occupational Therapy department.

While Kathy was giving me some tests, I asked, "By the way, where do you live?"

She gave me a wild answer, "On a street close to the hospital."

So I left the hospital and went to the Majik Market to call a friend, and just happened to look her up in the phone book. I noticed that she lived on Bransford Road where Fred lived.

When I got home that night I looked in the Augusta addresses and found out that Fred was Kathy's next door neighbor and they had never met!

So, I thought to myself, "It would be great for Fred to start a relationship with Kathy, and that would solve everything."

At Thanksgiving I told Fred all about Kathy. He was in Macon at that time, but told me he was going to Augusta to take a test, then would go next door to see her.

He went over there and told Kathy, "I am Gary Mann's first cousin."

After two weeks I began to wonder about that visit and how they liked each other. So, at Christmas, I wrote Fred a little note and gave it to him at our family get-together in Macon. The note said:

*To Dr. Freddy Daniel, M. D.*

*I know that I am too young for Kathy, so as a Christmas gift, I will let you have her. Maybe you will find that Kathy will make a lovely wife for you. I will be happy to be your best man at your wedding.*

*Your cousin,*
*Garo*

Then Fred put the note in his pocket and tried to change the subject. "Maybe you are not too young," he said.

I went back to Augusta for some more tests. Kathy was there and gave me a big kiss on my neck. All during my testing she was looking at me very sweetly, and I was looking at her very sweetly too. When I was walking out of the door, she was singing something. It sounded like "Close to You."

In two months I went back to Augusta for a special appointment, and Fred came over. He had to cut one of his classes to come to the auditorium, where my case was presented to the audience. Dr. Allen had made videos of me before and after surgery, and showed the before and after tapes to seventy-five visiting neurosurgeons, who were chiefs of Neurosurgery of medical schools from all over the country. The videos showed that I was better after the surgery. Then the visiting doctors wanted to personally see me in action, so Dr. Allen called me in front, and I walked, talked, and did coordination exercises.

After that I went by to see Kathy, but she was out sick. I was sorry to miss her, because I had wanted to see her, and because I had brought a red rose to give her. I had won the rose for dancing at a Valentine banquet several days earlier. I asked one the other therapists to please put the rose on Kathy's desk and be sure she got it. This lady promised she would.

Fred came to Macon after that. He told me he had asked Kathy for a date, but she said she was busy.

I told him that she was of a different religion and he said, "I know, but I do not think that is the reason."

Then he said she was upset from breaking up with a boyfriend.

Since Kathy was an awful letter writer, I asked Fred to really get on her about it. I had thought of an occupational therapist as a good writer, since therapists write up their patients and write up their treatments, but I was wrong about that.

In a few weeks I got a lengthy letter from Kathy. She wrote that she had made a big decision in her life, that she was moving to Boston. When I called her long distance, she said she would like to see me before she left Augusta. I told her that I was coming over there soon to see Fred, but we probably could not meet, as she would be visiting her parents in Jacksonville, Florida, on those dates, and she was involved with a wedding there on the Sunday that I was going to be Augusta. Anyway, I caught the bus early Sunday morning and went to Augusta.

I got there about eleven o'clock and Fred met me at the bus station. When we got to his apartment there were his girlfriend and her sister. We did a lot in twenty-two hours in Augusta! We ate lunch at Arby's, went fishing and caught three bass, had a fish fry, saw and talked to an old friend, went to see *Saturday Night Fever* with John Travolta, and tried to talk to Kathy on the phone, but she was not back in town yet.

Kathy got back home late that Sunday night, and she called me after midnight, and we talked for a long time. I had written out questions for Fred to ask her, as she could understand him better than me, and Fred wrote down her answers. It was so late and she was so tired that I did not have the heart to make her come by and see me, because she was a long way away at a friend's home in North Augusta, South Carolina. So, we said our good-byes on the phone.

Both of us were sad not to be able to see each other. She told me that she would write and send me a picture of herself. When she said she was going to write me, that did not mean a thing, because, as I mentioned before, she is an awful letter writer. But I kept checking the mailbox every day anyway.

While I was on my vacation at Sea Island, Georgia, I called her father in nearby Jacksonville.

He was very friendly and said, "She just found an apartment in Brookline, Massachusetts. She is not working yet, but is loving being lazy."

Many years have passed and I have never heard from Kathy again.

## Chapter 25

# *Meeting Billy in Carter Country*

It was just like any small town in the South. Arriving there about 11:30 in the morning, we went straight to the main attraction. It was just a plain old rundown place where the men hang around and tourists gather—none other than Billy Carter's service station.

On this special day, December 10, 1977, my father, my mother, my cousin Lyn Gibson, and I went to the famous town of Plains, Georgia, home of Jimmy Carter, president of the United States. We took the popular tour of Plains. We drove by the softball field, the hospital, Jimmy's school, Amy's old school, Miss Lillian's home, Billy's old home, Plains Baptist Church, the peanut warehouse, and a few other places.

At the service station before the tour, I bought some "Billy Beer" and found out that it tasted like any other.

Since my mother loves antiques, we looked up Hugh Carter's antique store. We met Hugh Carter himself. He talked to us a long time and was very friendly.

Then we drove out a mile to the "Plains Country Club." It was on the highway, but it was so small we passed by it at first. When we came back, and knocked on the side door, we heard somebody call, "Come in."

Opening the door, we were surprised to see Billy Carter sitting there drinking a "Billy Beer"! He was very friendly and said that he used to manage a paint store on Ingleside Avenue in Macon.

When I shot more than 42,000 on the pinball machine, Billy said, "Say, that's a good score! Not many make that high!"

He told us good-bye and wished me well. We had visited with him fifteen minutes and found him just a regular fellow.

## Chapter 26

# *The Day I Became an Uncle*

My father had just left for the hospital and my mother and I were just leaving for school when the phone rang at 8:00 a.m. It was my brother-in-law saying that my sister Beverly had been in labor since 5:30 that morning, January 4, 1978.

So, after locating my father and calling a few friends and kinfolks, we got ready to go to Marietta (a suburb of Atlanta). By 11:00 we were at the Kennestone Hospital. We asked where the fathers' waiting room was. A nurse told us that it was on the second floor. There we found David Chance, Beverly's husband, waiting in the hall.

When my mother and David went into the labor room, someone else in the hall asked me, "Is your wife having a baby?"

I replied, "No, but my sister is." That statement made me feel so old!

Beverly had told our father, a doctor, that she wanted him in the delivery room for the birth of her baby, but her obstetrician said no.

We waited all day in the fathers' waiting room, watching TV. There were about four other fathers-to-be, plus a handful of grandparents and their children, in that small room. After more than five hours of waiting, at 5:46 p.m. Daniel DeWitt Chance was born by Caesarian section. He weighed six pounds and nine ounces and was nineteen inches long. After that, we took the new father for a quick supper at the nearest Burger King, because we had to rush back to see Beverly before we went back to Macon that night.

We went back to see Beverly, David, and Daniel the next weekend. We went by the hospital on Saturday to see Beverly and Daniel before spending the night at their house. Today Daniel is a teenager. He is a good student and is very sports minded.

# Chapter 27

## *Stay on Your Side!*

After I had recovered from my brain pacemaker surgery, my father said, "Gary, it is time for you to learn how to drive a car."

I was a little afraid of the idea of having full control of a car, because I know so many people get killed when they are at the wheel of automobiles. Every day newspapers tell of deaths due to automobile accidents.

At first I drove on backcountry and dirt roads, so that I would not be in heavy traffic while I was getting the feel of the car. Then I had some fun, driving around the Macon Coliseum, doing big curves in the parking lot. Also, I practiced at Central City Park many times.

One day I was at my brother Clark's farmhouse, where he then lived. After a heavy rain, we went down a couple of miles to a field. I was trying to drive, but it got too muddy for me, so Clark took over. But then we almost fell into a big hole. Then we got stuck in the mud. Finally, we got out and made it back home. That taught me how hard it is to drive a car when it is not on a road.

A sure thing I learned was to stay on my side and in the middle of my lane. If I drove too far to the right I would almost run down the mailboxes. If I moved too far to the left I would cross the center line.

By now I was getting more relaxed behind the wheel and pretty good at driving. It was time to apply for my learner's license, so I went down to the Public Safety Department. Not having known that I would have to take a written test to get a learner's license, I took the test before I had ever read the driving handbook. Of course I failed it. My father and I were surprised, though, at how well I did.

I went home and really studied that handbook, to make sure that I would be able to pass next time. In two weeks I went back, and this time I passed my driving test.

After I had finished my test the officer questioned me. I thought I gave good answers to his questions, but he still had reservations about giving me a learner's license, because of my handicap. So my father wrote Dr. Allen for a letter of recommendation. Dr. Allen sent a statement to the Georgia State Patrol that it was okay for them to issue me a license. Less than a week later it was in my back pocket.

In order to make my driving better than he could alone, my father had Lt. Slye and Sgt. Joiner of the Macon Police Department give me private lessons. Now I am driving all over the city and sometimes the highway, but always with another licensed adult driver in the front seat. I have learned to stay on my side. The reason I never drive alone is because, if I were ever involved in an accident, I might be blamed, just because I have cerebral palsy. One day I hope to overcome that and be able to get a full license.

## Chapter 28

# *Jennie*

In the fall quarter of my senior year in high school I took a "Famous Americans" course. There I found a sweet sixteen-year-old girl with long brown hair named Jennie. She sat by me in class.

Since she refused to give me her phone number or even her address, I decided to outfox her.

I wrote a note saying, "Do you know Jennie and where does she live?"

I showed it to everybody I knew. But she wrote me a note saying that I was a sweet guy but she would like for us to be just friends.

It was not long before I found out that my Geometry teacher had taken care of Jenny when she was small. So this teacher told me a lot about Jennie and gave me her address.

At first I was going to call her without any warning that I had found out where she lived. But I did not want her to have a heart attack, so I gave her a big hint, which helped her guess my source of information.

One night we talked on the phone a long time and decided to go to see the movie *Hooper*, starring Burt Reynolds. Both of us enjoyed it very much. After the movie we went for a pizza. There I found out that Jennie had been a ballet dancer for ten years. She had danced in *The Nutcracker Suite* several times. I went with her one day to ballet practice and saw her doing some dance routines. Jennie was interested in disco dancing, too.

Besides going to the movie, pizza place, and ballet, I had Jennie over to my house several times. Once when I was having a birthday supper, we played a game of pinball and I beat the socks off her. The score was something like 1,500 to 300. She must have never played a pinball machine in her life!

By that time Jennie and I had become real close to each other. We were not sweethearts, but just brothers and sisters in Christ, as we are both Christians. Both of us had other people that we dated, but I accepted that.

Jennie was in my Biology class in the spring quarter of 1979. We are just friends and I am very happy to have had her as my "sister." I have only seen Jennie a few times since high school, but she was my date for one college fraternity party a year or so later.

## Chapter 29

# *Putting It All Together*

In the fall of 1978 I realized that the end of my sixteen years in the Macon public school system was nearing, because high school graduation was approaching. It had been hard for me to get a regular education because of my physical handicaps. But, many things that people had said I would never be able to do, I had done. They said that if I worked in a regular classroom I would be made fun of. Also, they thought I might get beaten up by tough boys, knocked down in the hallways, and tripped up in the lunchroom. But when I was finally let into regular classes in the eighth grade, none of these things ever happened. Now I was about to complete the twelfth grade and graduate!

I was at the Lanier part of the Central Complex for my third and last year, having attended the eighth and ninth grades at Ballard B, as already described. From the tenth grade on I had gone to Lanier High School, and I considered it to be one of the finest public high schools in the nation. I really flipped over this school and all its teachers.

At this senior high school I had the good fortune to be in the classes of many fine teachers, including Mr. Gus Johnson, about whom I have written in a previous chapter.

Another favorite was our librarian Mrs. Frances Harrison. She and I became friends, as well as colleagues. One day in my sophomore year a sudden storm came up, and within two hours Macon was covered with a four-inch blanket of snow. I was in the library when the school closed due to he weather, as Macon is so unused to and unprepared for snow, which seldom falls here. Mrs. Harrison tried to take me to her house in her car, since I lived in the same neighborhood. Then, on arrival at her house, she planned to call Mother to come the few blocks to get me. But we got stuck in the snow on the way. So a man in a four-wheel drive Jeep had to get me out of Mrs. Harrison's car and drive me home. But Mrs. Harrison walked home through the snow!

Another of my teachers was the crazy and wild band director Bob Barnette. He was the award-winning director of the Central Sugar Bear marching band and also a music teacher. Since he was so way-out, I nicknamed him "Bobby Baby." To show how wild he was, one time, to help the band, he was the rat on top of the dunking machine. I bought four balls for a dollar. I missed two times in a row, but then I poked the bull's-eye with the end of my cane, and plunged him into the cold water.

Two years later I took over and led his band at a Christmas special concert at Lanier. This exploit got me on the TV news. It was the last day before our Christmas holidays. I felt honored that Bob had asked me to lead the band. Bob introduced me by telling the audience how close our friendship was. All of the students gave me a standing ovation.

Three months later I took a music appreciation course from Bobby Baby. He was an unusual teacher. He would always bring a toy electronic football game to class. Sometimes between lessons he would play this game. One night Bobby Baby came to my house and we played a few games of pinball. It was a pretty even match.

In the spring quarter of my senior year I was really looking forward to my graduation from Central. I ordered my announcements and sent them out. It was about three weeks before the big graduation night. My overall grade for all my high school years was a high B, and I was in the upper twenty-five percent of the class! I received a lot of gifts during that time.

The great occasion finally arrived, and I started to get a little bit nervous. I had been assigned two seats in the Macon Coliseum. The one on the front row on the right, facing the stage, was to sit in before I went on stage, and the other, on the left, was to sit in after receiving the diploma.

The graduation ceremonies finally started. I felt uncomfortable in my white robe and rented shoes, and it was very hot that June day of 1979. When the name "Gary Edward Mann" was called, I climbed the right-hand stairs, walked to the middle of the stage, got my diploma, then walked to the left and down the stairs to my reserved seat. While I was doing this the whole student body, the 309 graduating seniors, and the faculty stood and applauded. Then the entire Coliseum audience of about 2,000 people joined in, standing and clapping too. It was a wonderful feeling to see that that many people realized how hard I had had to work to graduate, and to me this showed they had been with me all the way. It was a great night!

After that big evening, I went to work in the business office at one of the local hospitals. I worked during the summer for ten weeks, and liked my job and coworkers, and I enjoyed receiving a modest paycheck.

# Chapter 30

# *First Year in College*

In late 1978, in my last year of high school, I started thinking about where I might go to college. I rapidly boiled down the list to two possibilities: Emory University in Atlanta or Mercer University in Macon. At that time I was wondering if I might be able to go to regular undergraduate school, then to Candler School of Theology at Emory, to become a preacher like my late grandfather.

So it seemed like maybe a good idea to go to Emory for both types of education. We made an appointment with Dr. Laney, the dean of Emory, in early 1979. We went to see him and he was very kind. He said my high school grades were good enough for Emory to accept me, and he assured me that his school was particularly responsive and caring for the handicapped. He stated that if a handicapped student at Emory were physically unable to attend the class he wanted in the building it was in, that the class would be brought to him.

A little later I went to see Dr. John Mitchell, the admissions head officer of Mercer. He seemed even more enthusiastic about my possible enrollment at Mercer than Dr. Laney had been about Emory. Dr. Mitchell charmed me with his caring attitude. After much thought, I realized how much I depended on my parents. I decided on Mercer, and that I would just continue to live at home, and commute to school, right at first anyway.

So in September 1979 I began classes at Mercer University as a freshman. But, starting two weeks prior to that official opening date, I had been invited to participate in a special program called "Opportunity Scholars." This program was designed to help new students with irregular backgrounds to adjust to college life. I went through this program, and it was very good for me. I met some nice professors, who showed me the campus, and taught me some good general information. Also I met many fine people in this program who also were entering the freshman class.

When regular fall quarter started, the campus was flooded with many more students. I was anxious to make friends with people from other places.

My father had told me to look for another new student, from LaGrange, Georgia, who was the son of one of his medical school classmates. I found this boy on campus. He said his name was Chad Turner. I soon found him to be a great fellow.

He said to me over and over again, "We are going to be fraternity brothers, because our fathers were in medical school together."

Two weeks after that we did become fraternity brothers!

The first week of classes was very rushed, with much excitement. I selected my three courses, which was the standard work load, went to these classes, and met my professors. Mostly they seemed quite different from the teachers I had had in high school. I wondered if I would be able to do all the assignments they started handing out.

Another early concern was fraternity rush. All male students indicated whether or not they wanted to go out for fraternity rush; female students did the same for sororities. The week after classes started I signed up for rush. Since my father had been a Kappa Alpha at Mercer, I knew I wanted to be one too, if possible.

I went through rush like everyone else. We were required to visit all eight fraternity houses on the Mercer campus. On the first night, as the university rules called for, I walked to four fraternity houses. The second night I visited the other four fraternities. On the third and last night of rush we were told to visit the three fraternities that we liked best. It was raining every night that I went to the fraternity houses. It seems to rain at Mercer every year during rush. Walking in the rain dressed in a coat and tie was not much fun. After this, and after going to several rush parties, Kappa Chapter of the Kappa Alpha Order gave me a bid. I accepted and became a pledge. The date was October 5, 1979. I was very happy about the whole thing.

Just the satisfaction of knowing the brothers liked and wanted me, in spite of my physical handicap, was most gratifying. My parents were also very glad that I had been offered this bid. I did not know it then, but this fraternity would offer me the opportunity to make many lifelong friends.

I especially liked the idea that the KA fraternity emphasized the importance of being a gentleman and respecting the ladies at all times. In fact, the motto of the fraternity is *Dieu et les Dames.*

One of the requirements of pledges for Mondays was to wear a tie to all classes. It was fun for me because people paid me a bit more attention, as a student wearing a tie and coat was unusual. My Biology professor, Louise Morgan, told me that she always looked forward to Mondays to see me in a coat and tie.

Several other professors asked me, "Are you preaching tonight?"

After finishing classes each day I did some of my homework in the Learning Skills Center. The center was a place where students could go to seek help in a particular subject and to work individually. That first quarter of college I started taking Biology, with a lab two days a week, and History and English. After two weeks of carrying a full load, the director of the Learning Skills Center, Pam, told me the I was overworked and had better drop a course before I had a nervous breakdown. Since I had failed two of my History tests, I decided to drop that subject. I kept taking English and Biology. After I had worked in the Learning Skills Center a few months, I named it "The Lab."

Every Wednesday Mercer held no classes. This was called "Wonderful Wednesday." Because it was so popular with students, it was believed to be a cause of increased enrollment at Mercer. I spent Wednesdays catching up on my reading and homework. On Tuesday nights the K.A.s would have a beer party. I never drank more than two beers at a party, but some pledges or brothers did, so they were glad they did not have to go to school the next day!

With my reduced load of two courses, I passed the first quarter without too much trouble. It was hard for me to learn all the strange biology terms. But I made good in it. My advisors, the learning center, my professors, and my K.A. buddies all helped me.

The second quarter of Mercer I took two subjects again. Again I made successful grades. I had to study a lot, but I liked doing that. But the second quarter is never a very happy one, due to the cold and rainy weather, which gives everyone the blues. Most of my fellow pledges had been initiated into K.A. late in the fall, but I had been sick then, so my time had to be postponed until later. My ceremony was held in the Spring. At the end of the initiation, I was surprised to find that my father had been there throughout the entire proceedings. The date I become a brother was March 26, 1980. I cannot tell any details of the initiation rites, as they are secret, but this was a very special occasion for me.

Shortly after my initiation, all of the brothers became busy getting ready for the yearly "Old South" week, a week of nonstop partying, which is always held in April. I asked a student writer/tutor, Suzi Margolin, who worked in the lab, to be my date for the week. Suzi had beautiful curly hair and an olive skin. She was from Los Angeles and had an interesting background. She had been in school with Kami Colter and Micheal Learned's son, and had known all of the cast of "The Waltons" TV series. One of Suzi's cousins is movie actress Janet Margolin. Suzi agreed to be my date.

The highlight of the Old South week is the Old South Ball. The morning of the ball some of us went to the mayor's office at City Hall in our Confederate uniforms to let him declare Friday as "Old South Day." All of the men wore Confederate uniforms to the ball, and the women wore *Gone With the Wind*-type hoopskirted dresses. Suzi borrowed the hoop for her dress from Mrs. Morgan, the biology professor.

Suzi and I double-dated with Chad and his date. I had always thought that I was a fast dancer, but I could not keep up with Suzi on the dance floor. We had a great time and got in about 1:15 a.m.

After that big event, I started worrying whether I would pass Political Science, which was one of my two courses that third (spring) quarter. The hardest professor on campus taught it. I thought I would probably do all right, since politics is one of my favorite interests. But I remained unsure of receiving a passing grade. One of my K.A. brothers started coaching me three times a week. He was in my class, along with four other K.A.s. Bryan helped me understand it better. With his help, and by asking the professor some questions during class, I did make a passing grade. I also passed my other subject.

As a reward for finishing my first year in college without failing any subject or having a nervous breakdown, my father gave me a specially ordered Kappa Alpha Order Bulova Accutron wristwatch.

Summer was just around the corner, and I started thinking about going to regular Mercer summer school to take Environmental Science during the first session.

But before I signed up, I got a letter from the Human Services Department of the school saying, "If you work at least twenty hours a week for ten weeks in the field of Human Service during this summer, you can receive ten hours of college credit."

That sounded good to me. The summer prior to coming to Mercer I had worked in the business office of the Medical Center of Central Georgia. So my mother talked to the boss there, and he said he knew about this CETA (Comprehensive Employment and Training Act) program, and that he would be happy to have me back again that summer, and for Mercer credit as well as for the same pay.

I went to the professor in charge of the program, Dr. Thomas Glennon, who approved this plan. In addition to working at the hospital, Dr. Glennon assigned me two books to read and to write reports on. So that summer I worked at the hospital four hours a day for ten weeks, and read the books and wrote the required reports. The best thing about this whole deal was that I made two A's.

So I felt that my first twelve months at Mercer had been successful.

## Chapter 31

# *"Professor Gary Mann"*

To my surprise, I was asked to do something I had never dreamed of doing. It was in the summer between high school and my freshman year at Mercer. Dr. Richard Logan asked me to speak to one of his Special Education classes at Mercer. One of my favorite things for sure is talking. I will state my ideas as long as people will listen. But because of my speech handicap, I never thought anyone would ask me to speak before a class.

Dr. Richard Logan had been my speech teacher most of the time since I was fourteen, and we grew to be very close friends during the years. I could discuss just about anything with him.

Richard came by my house and picked me up for my first lecture to a class of undergraduate Education students. I was a bit nervous about talking in front of a group of people, but I just acted as myself, and all was fine. The lecture was during the first session of summer school. I wore one of my five Mercer shirts, so I would feel a real part of the university. For high school graduation, some people, knowing about my going to Mercer, had given me Mercer University T-shirts.

At this first lecture I stood in the front of a room filled with twenty-five students majoring in Education. Richard told me that there are two most important things to lecturing. The first is to use good eye contact with your audience. The other is to use the most understandable speech possible. After I gave my talk, Richard said I did very well.

Then, in September 1979, the first quarter of my freshman year at Mercer had started. Richard asked me to lecture again, this time to one of his Special Education classes. I used the same talk as before. In both lectures I told some general things about myself, I asked the students what some of their handicaps were, and ended up by taking questions from the floor. The students were surprised that I thought everyone had some kind of handicap, but were soon able to discover some in themselves. Richard told me that I did better the second time. He asked me to lecture several more times at Mercer, and I improved with each speech.

Then Richard introduced me to his neighbor, Dr. Don Midkiff, who happened to be an Education professor at Mercer. Dr. Midkiff had just moved from Virginia during my freshman year. Later I attended a Thanksgiving church service where he sang the evening solo. We had further contacts and became friends. Since the name Midkiff was hard for me to pronounce, I searched for an easy nickname. I came up with "Dr. Don."

I told Dr. Don that I was a guest lecturer in Special Education, and would be happy to talk to one of his classes. A few months later he told me that some of his students were majoring in the field of Special Education, and he invited me to talk to them.

By now I was getting to feel like a college professor and thought I should look more professional. My new look was a navy blue shirt with a buttoned down collar and a blue striped tie. I made an outline of my lecture to pass out, for students to follow as I was speaking. Now Professor Mann was ready to lecture to Dr. Don's class. Only twenty students were in the room and they were quieter than those in Richard's classes. I received only a question or two. Richard's students usually asked four or five.

I had greatly admired my grandfather Rev. David G. Mann, and wanted to follow in his footsteps. Even though I had decided on Mercer, in my hometown, for the first two years of college, at first I was planning to transfer to Emory about my junior year, for further study in some religious field. I was hoping to get my undergraduate degree from Emory, and then go on to the Candler School of Theology at Emory. So at Mercer I had started off majoring in Christianity.

At the beginning of my second year at Mercer, Richard took the position of head of the Education Department of Wesleyan College, also in Macon. Wesleyan is an almost all-female school. Again he asked me to speak. The Wesleyan class had ten cute girls in it who asked me a lot of questions. Richard said my speech was my best ever, but I needed to work on my eye contact.

Since I had then lectured four times at Mercer for Richard, once for Dr. Don, and once again for Richard at Wesleyan, I thought I should start charging for my talks. I considered writing a letter to Mercer and Wesleyan suggesting that I be put on their payrolls. Since I had been enjoying lecturing to Education students, mostly those in Special Education, I began seriously thinking about maybe changing my major from Christianity to Education, probably specializing in Special Education. I was even thinking about possibly getting my Ph.D. in that field!

# Chapter 32

## *Big Brother, Little Brother*

After being in Kappa Alpha Order for a year, I started wondering about whom I would get for a "Little Brother." All K.A. sophomores would get freshmen Little Brothers.

In my mind a lot of questions were forming: Will he be a Christian? Will be worship alcohol? Will he accept me having cerebral palsy?

On one Friday afternoon a tall, good-looking freshman with black hair came up to me. We talked for awhile and he said he was Mark Brittain.

After we had been talking for about fifteen minutes he said, "I am your K.A. 'Little Brother'."

Mark made the ideal Little Brother because he was a Christian, he did not drink a lot, and he was a fine dresser and very much a Southern gentleman. When he first came to my house Mark called my mother "Darling," and I was very shocked. Later I found out he likes ladies and calls a lot of them that. Women like it because Mark is better looking than Burt Reynolds or Robert Redford.

Mark liked to listen to religious music on his car tape player. One day he and I were out at the Macon Mall singing religious songs as we walked. People stared at us, while we just went on walking and singing.

We made a deal that every time we went out to supper we would take turns paying for it. After supper Mark would always stop for some ice cream. That suited me fine, because I love ice cream too. One of our favorite places to eat was at Skipper's, a seafood restaurant. Skipper Zimmerman, the owner, used to live in my neighborhood, and is a close friend to my family. Another time Mark and I were very hungry, and we decided to go to a Wendy's. But we got to a Burger King first. When Mark and I walked in, I had a Wendy on my mind. I tried to order a Wendy from a Burger King! Mark said, "You're lucky they didn't shoot you."

Mark asked me to call him at his home in Atlanta whenever I might be up there during our six-week Christmas vacation. My family often goes to Atlanta, less than one hundred miles away. So, during Christmas holidays, the first time I was in Atlanta, we did call him. My mother and I met Mark and his mother for lunch. He is very close to his mother because his father died when he was just eight years old. Mark has a sister who has a young son, whom Mark loves and treats as his own.

Mark would often go with me to my church, even though he is a Baptist and I am a Methodist. We went to a new Sunday School class for college-age people for a few Sundays. He enjoyed listening to my minister. After church we would go out to lunch with my parents.

By now, Mark told me he would like for me to meet his girlfriend Merrilee. She was a student at University of Georgia in Athens then. Merrilee and Mark had gone to the same high school near Atlanta, but had only met their senior year.

The K.A. Old South Week was right around the corner and Mark told me he was planning to have Merrilee come down to Macon from Athens for the ball. This year my parents had agreed to host the big annual K.A. cocktail party at our home on the afternoon of the Ball that night. The cocktail party and the Ball were both scheduled for the Friday after April Fools' Day.

I thought up a great April Fools' joke to play on Mark.

On April first I called him and announced, "Mark, I hate to tell you this, but the K.A. president has called off the cocktail party, because the chapter can't afford it."

Mark thought I was crying when I was saying it, but I was laughing. When he realized I was joking he said, "I will get you back for that."

Throughout all of Old South Week we rode in Mark's mother's red Cadillac convertible with the top down. Before the cocktail party we were in a parade in this fancy car. Also in the car were Merrilee, as Mark's date, Belinda, with me, and four K.A. Roses (pretty fraternity sponsors).

Being with Mark my sophomore year was one of the happiest times I had in the Kappa Chapter of the Kappa Alpha Order. One of my biggest surprises was a paddle with the signatures of all of the K.A. brothers and pledges, given to me by Mark. He had made it himself, with a K.A. crest on one side. It is still in my possession and I treasure it.

A few years later, when he was in law school in Birmingham, Mark got even with me with a real good April Fools' joke.

His wife sent me a telegram that said:

> GARY, EMERGENCY. MARK KICKED OUT OF SCHOOL—IS DRUNK AND UNMANAGEABLE. CALL IMMEDIATELY.

I fell for it. But, of course, it was only a joke.

Today, Mark is a successful attorney in McDonough, Georgia. He is married to a fun-loving lady named Connie. Mark and Connie have three children named Jackie, Jamie, and Jordan.

# Chapter 33

## *My Special Friend*

During my second year at Mercer, 1980–1981, I again lived at home and commuted. All three quarters I took only two courses. Even though I had received ten hours of college credit during the summer, I was already getting a little behind, due to this reduced work load. I knew it would take me at least five or six years to complete my college education, but that was okay with me. I continued to work hard, and was able to pass everything. I remained much involved with extracurricular activities, mostly those of my fraternity. I also was very interested in the social life, and especially in *girls*!

During this second year I became more friendly with Belinda. I had met her originally at the Opportunity Scholar program both of us had been in the previous year just before starting regular classes. This young lady caught my eye at that time. She was very sweet, pretty, and athletic. Her full name was Belinda Lee Frost.

When I asked where she was from, Belinda would say, "I am from the 'boondocks' of Columbus, Georgia."

Belinda was the manager of the "Teddy Bears" girls' basketball team at the university. She was on the road with the team a lot during our freshman year, so we were not too close then. However, during our second year at Mercer, we saw each other more. Sometimes she would hold my arm and walk me across the campus, because I am a slow walker.

By now, Belinda became one of my closest friends. She told me that I was a special person to her. I enjoyed hearing her talk about her life. Belinda was the youngest child in her family, with several brothers and sisters much older than she. Since her mother worked and was gone all day, Belinda had been raised at home mostly by her father, who had retired early on disability.

When small, Belinda thought of her neighbor Kevin as a big brother. He lived across the street and was eight years older than she. When she got in high school he was her basketball coach.

Teasingly Kevin would say, "Someday, when you grow up, I'm going to marry you."

Belinda thought, "He's too old for me."

It was time for the yearly fraternity convivium (banquet). This event honors the birthday of General Robert E. Lee, who was the spiritual founder of the Kappa Alpha Order. I invited Belinda to a party at the K.A. mansion, and she accepted. She enjoyed meeting my little brother Mark and the other brothers. We had lots of fun that night.

The Old South week-long party was just around the corner. It was easy for me to decide whom I wanted my date to be, Belinda. I asked her, and she told me that she would be honored to be my date and to let me escort her for the week. Before the Old South Ball (as described above, in the previous chapter), my parents had invited all the K.A.s and their dates to a cocktail party in our home and on the grounds.

Of all the girls there, Belinda, with her long black hair, was the prettiest. She looked wonderful in her red and white dotted swiss hoop-skirted dress, with a red ribbon sash around her waist. K.A. had hired a photographer, who took many pictures. One was of Belinda and me sitting on our love seat in the living room. It was one of her favorite pieces of furniture in my house. Belinda brought my mother a dozen red roses to show her appreciation for letting her use the dress and hoop skirt. (We we had borrowed the dress from mother's friend Marguerite Cato and the hoop skirt from my biology professor Louise Morgan.) Also Belinda assisted us in entertaining the 200 guests.

Right after the Old South celebration, Belinda helped me with an Education course. The main thing I needed help in was to write a book report on *Goodbye, Mr. Chips*. I finally finished the paper, but my mind was a little bit more on Belinda.

Belinda and I said that we would write each other during the three-month summer break. She went to spend the summer with her parents, who had retired to Melbourne Beach, Florida. I did more letter writing than Belinda, so after not receiving a line, I sent her a self-addressed stamped envelope, and got a letter back in a week.

At the end of fall quarter the following year, Belinda transferred from Mercer because of personal matters. She enrolled in a college near Melbourne. I was very upset that one of my best friends had left Mercer. But we kept in touch, mostly by calling each other long distance. Also, Belinda wrote me several letters and I answered them.

The following March, during spring break, my family and I took a trip to Vero Beach, Florida, to visit my brother Clark, who lived there at that time. I thought maybe we could see Belinda, because Melbourne is only thirty miles north of Vero. Everything worked out so this could happen. She came to our Oceanside Inn Motel and spent the day with us. We had lunch at the Driftwood Motel next door, and sunned on the beach. That night Belinda and I went to a good movie, *On Golden Pond.* She especially liked my little nephew Daniel, who was with us. Daniel was four years old then. And he fell for her too. I was very honored that Belinda had taken the time to make me a gift, a needlepoint pillow with bright red roses on it. The pillow is beautiful and will be special to me forever.

Belinda came back to Mercer that May for her former roommate's wedding. She brought me some very big news.

Belinda asked me, "Remember that boy, Kevin, my neighbor in Columbus, who coached me in high school basketball, and who always joked that he would marry me when I grew up? Well, he and I are getting married on June 27, 1982, at the Fort Benning chapel, right outside Columbus!"

I was very shocked! Belinda invited me to the wedding and to sit with her family.

One of the reasons my friendship with Belinda was so special was because she lost a brother in a drowning accident during her sophomore year at Mercer.

After that happened, Belinda said, "You are my adopted big brother."

I thought the engagement between Belinda and Kevin was a very happy fantasy come true. The only thing I was concerned about was that

Belinda would be moving to Germany, where Kevin was stationed. He was serving there with the U.S. Army, and worked in the intelligence office.

My father and mother were involved with a dinner party and could not take me to the wedding. Belinda told me that she would be hurt if I missed her big event. I called my step-grandmother, Clariece, in Columbus. She invited me to spend the night with her.

So I bought a ticket and rode the bus to Columbus. A friend of Clariece's took me to Fort Benning to the wedding. Belinda introduced me to Kevin about five minutes before the ceremony. She was a beautiful bride and the whole service was lovely. I was proud to sit with her parents.

After the wedding, Belinda's father and mother cooked a delicious dinner for their guests. Later on that night, the father of the bride took me back to Clariece's apartment.

Saying good-bye to my special friend Belinda was a very hard thing to do.

Belinda and Kevin are divorced now. She is living in the Orlando area with her son Gabe. The last time that we talked to each other was quite a few years ago, on the phone.

## Chapter 34

# *My Adventure in New England*

At the end of my second year at Mercer, in May 1981, I again looked for a summer job. Again I was able to work at the big city hospital for twenty hours a week for ten weeks for the same pay. As I had done the previous summer, with book reports and other requirements, I was able to get ten more hours of Mercer credit. But we had a big trip planned for that summer. Fortunately, my bosses let me get off for those days, to be made up later.

On July 10 my mother, my father, and I drove to the Atlanta Airport, at that time the world's largest, to fly to Washington, D.C. Also along on the trip were two cousins, Jane McKissack and her daughter Kim, for a journey to the nation's capital, Boston, and Cape Cod. When I walked through the airport check-in and metal detector, my brain pacemaker and metal chest electrode sounded off so they thought I was an armed robber or a hijacker! But the guards understood when we explained. We boarded Delta Jet flight 528 and landed at the Washington National Airport in a little more than an hour.

When we got settled in the Quality Inn at Pentagon City in Arlington, Virginia, I called my first cousin Hal Mann, who works for the Navy in Washington. He came out to our place for a few hours. We had dinner in the restaurant in the revolving dome on top of our motel. From there we had a great view of Washington at night.

The next day was Saturday. We waited in a three-hour line to see the White House. It was a very long wait for a short tour of the Red, Blue, Green, and Gold rooms. I bought a book about the First Family's house. Then followed a trip to the old Smithsonion Institution and to the Air and

Space Museum. I saw interesting things in both places, but in the latter I especially enjoyed seeing every type aircraft from the first plane the Wright Brothers flew to the capsule from the first journey to the moon. After lunch, Jane, Kim, and my mother went to the National Gallery of Art and the Museum of Natural History, while Daddy and I went to the National Archives that houses the United States Constitution, the Bill of Rights, the Declaration of Independence, important papers of George Washington, and other historical documents. They say in case of a bomb hitting Washington the documents will be lowered into the ground. All of the documents were hard to read because they were under double glass for protection.

Sunday was our last full day in the Capitol City, so we toured the Lincoln Memorial, Jefferson Memorial, and a few other places. One of the best things about Washington was the sightseeing tourmobile, because you could ride on it all day or for as long as you wanted for a low fee. The guides told the passengers what all of the buildings were. The tourmobile let all of us off at the Arlington Cemetery, and we took another tourmobile to the Kennedy brothers' tombs, Robert E. Lee's home, and the Changing of the Guard. The Changing of the Guard was very impressive to me because the guards are on duty guarding the Tomb of the Unknown Soldier twenty-four hours a day, seven days a week, fifty-two weeks a year.

We went back to our hotel to pack up for Boston. The flight was short and a little bit rough, but the Delta snacks were great. When we arrived in Boston, I discovered some facts about this city—that is was very old and dirty and had a lot of sorry drivers. We got a taxi to the Howard Johnson's in Cambridge. The neatest thing about that taxi ride was that we went two miles through a tunnel under the Charles River. That night we went on top of the John Hancock Observation Tower for a beautiful view of Boston in the early evening. It was one of the prettiest sights I had ever seen.

The next day we went on a sightseeing bus tour. I thought the driver had never driven in downtown Boston before, because he ran over corners and drove out of his lane. The tour was sorry, in that we did not go by half of the things we were supposed to see. The bus bypassed Paul

Revere's house that was listed as being on the tour. We got off the bus, and my mother, Jane, and Kim walked several blocks to Revere's two-story wooden house to take a picture of it.

Since taxis had very high prices, we rented a blue four-door Ford Fairmont with no air conditioning and a dirty windshield. It sounded as if the back end were coming apart. But it took us everywhere without any problem, and it was not very hot with the windows rolled down. We went to see the Charles River, which separates Cambridge from Boston, the campuses of the Massachusetts Institute of Technology and of Harvard, and a lot of other interesting places.

The next afternoon Daddy, Jane, Kim, and I went to the Suffolk Downs horse racing track. We watched eight races out of the nine, and bet a few times, but lost. Kim was especially interested in this activity, since she was planning to be a veterinarian. I enjoyed watching the races very much.

The next day we left in the car to drive to Hyannis on Cape Cod. On the way we stopped at Plymouth Rock, and it was very shocking to see how small the rock was. People have chipped a lot of it away. Plymouth Rock is about the size of the table in our breakfast room. My mother asked a lady where a good seafood place was. She told us to go to Souza's on the dock. We went there, and the lobster and shrimp were the best any of us had ever had.

After seeing Plymouth Rock, we drove on to our motel in Hyannis, where Daddy had a three-day medical meeting. The Dumfey Inn seemed a mile long, and our rooms were at the end of the building, so I had to walk a long way to get anywhere. Our stay there was a leisurely one of resting, shopping, and swimming.

But the last full day in Hyannis was a busy one. Kim and I had our portraits done in pastel by a local artist. Kim's picture turned out to be great, and mine was good but it made me look too serious. The next event of the day was a boat tour in Lewis and Hyannis Bays, that included going by the Kennedy residences, the site of the movie *Jaws*, and several other interesting landmarks.

That afternoon we went over to a house on the bay belonging to the sister of one of my former teachers, Bettye Parker. Bettye was there visiting at the time. Her sister gave us drinks and refreshments. The view from their house was beautiful. That night we took Bettye to see the play *The Pajama Game* in a big tent. It was very funny and I got the leading actor, John Raitt's, autograph.

The last morning of our New England trip was Kim's seventeenth birthday. We had a little celebration for her. On the way back to Boston from Hyannis we stopped again at Souza's for a last fresh seafood lunch, before driving to Logan Airport for a two-hour wait for the flight to Atlanta that Sunday evening. My adventure in New England was fantastic!

# Chapter 35

## *Living in the Dormitory*

In the fall of 1981 I began my third year at Mercer and decided it was time for me to move into a dormitory. At first I was a little anxious about leaving home and living at school instead, but I soon got used to the change.

My first roommate was a guy from Warner Robins, a town eighteen miles from Macon. He was a freshman who wanted to major in music. I told him I was a Kappa Alpha, and invited him to eat at the K.A. table in the dining hall. But after a few weeks he joined another fraternity.

That third year at Mercer I again signed up for two subjects, and started right in working hard on my lessons. I had new teachers and new subjects, and got along all right. By now, of course, I was familiar with the campus and everything that would be expected of me in class.

Other than with my schoolwork, I continued to be much involved with my fraternity and its activities, which remained a big part of my college life. At that time K.A. was the best fraternity on campus. There were several reasons why I believed Kappa Alpha was number one. K.A. is the only fraternity that has Robert E. Lee as its spiritual founder. Lee oversaw formation of the Kappa Alpha Order on December 21, 1865, on the campus of Washington College (now Washington and Lee University) in Lexington, Virginia, where he was president. Four students started K.A., mainly for brotherhood, but also to encourage young men to treat ladies as Southern gentlemen should. Although Lee is considered the fraternity's spiritual founder, of course he could not be a member of it, since he was president of the college rather than a student.

Almost every year during my Mercer time K.A. sold tickets for an expense-paid trip to the Bahamas for the winner of a drawing. You did not need to be a K.A. to win. The free Bahamas trip was a campus-wide campaign to help raise money for the Muscular Dystrophy Association. All of the tickets were put in a hat, and the last name drawn was that of the lucky winner. One year I won a trophy for suggesting, organizing, and helping put on a Dance-a-thon for muscular dystrophy. Also, in sports, K.A. won the interfraternity football championship in the fall of 1982.

While I was living on campus all of the K.A.s helped me when I needed a helping hand. The main thing I needed was for someone to carry my tray in the cafeteria, from the food line to the table. Brothers had ordered the pledges to always do this for me, but sometimes a pledge was hard to find. But someone would always carry the tray. All of the K.A.s would joke with me, and make remarks like, "You want two eggs, juice, milk, and Belinda." Belinda was my girlfriend then. Sometimes I would fool them and say I wanted pancakes or french toast.

After two courses a quarter for three years, I passed my subjects, but was only about half way toward a degree. In the Summer of 1982 I again worked, and tried to save most of my wages.

In September I went back into the dormitory again, and was assigned a new roommate, a fellow named Tim from Albany, Georgia. I believe that the Lord sent Tim to be my roommate because he was studying to be a Baptist preacher. We always got into arguments about which were better, Baptists or Methodists. We finally agreed that both are about equal. Tim was totally opposite from my first roommate. Now it was like living with "Mr. Clean" with a bottle of "Glass Plus." Tim moved out after two quarters, because he felt he needed a private room. As a roommate Tim got a ten on my number scale of one to ten, which was higher than I would rate my first roommate.

For my junior and senior years at Mercer, I had a private room in the dorm. I lived by myself and loved it.

One thing I learned as a K.A. brother during my years at Mercer was that there never was a dull moment. A very funny brother took the grand prize as the funniest K.A. alive, Ed Magruder. He told jokes seven days a week, twenty-four hours a day. He put pepper in my tea, tied my shoelaces together while I was on my feet, and put chewing gun in a chair and offered me a seat. Ed poured popcorn in my coke when we went to a movie. He did all of this to show that he really liked me. Ed only stayed at Mercer for two years, and I was a lucky man when he left.

In the winter of 1983 I was in a very hard class on Environmental Science. A lot of my K.A. brothers were also in it. The professor gave out so much information most students had to take four or five pages of notes daily. I used a tape recorder, but he talked so much the tape would run out before the class was over. I would always borrow notes from one of the K.A.s in the class, from Jim, Mike, Steve, or Bob. On the evening before the final exam, Jim was kind enough to help me study. And I did pass the course.

Another special thing took place that quarter. One of my classmates and a K.A. Rose, Jackie Laidlaw, won the title of "Miss Mercer" for 1983. When Jackie was named "Miss Mercer" I was so excited I almost had a heart attack. Jackie was in the "Miss Georgia" contest in June of that year, although not the winner there.

A few weeks into spring quarter, I began looking for an Old South date. I thought about a lady who had been in my Geology class in the fall. She had transferred to Mercer from Emory University. Her name was Judy. She was an Art Education major. At that time Judy wanted to go into art therapy, working with patients through their art.

Judy agreed to be my date, and we had a good time during Old South week. As usual there was a big K.A. parade in downtown Macon. That year the traditional cocktail party before the Ball was at the Dan Dunwody's beautiful home.

Because I only had a learner's drivers license and could not drive by myself, my K.A. brothers were good about taking me places. When I was living at home, a K.A. would always bring me back after meetings. Later, when I lived at Mercer, I remember one time Bryan Ellis took me on "Krystal run" after a fraternity meeting. We ordered four cheeseburgers each and went back to my dorm room to dig in.

Because of this feeling of real brotherhood and the fun we had together, I am very happy to have been a brother in the Kappa Alpha Order.

Also I have come to realize what a privilege it was to have gone to Mercer University. The professors and students were great to me. Ms. Mary Jane Pollitzer, in the Special Services Department of Mercer, furnished some tutors for me and for other special students in our early years there. And, since I could not take longhand notes rapidly due to cerebral palsy in my hands, I was given special permission to take to classes a voice-activated mini tape recorder to record the professors' lectures. At that time such instruments were very new, rare, and expensive. My father had to go to the wholesale southeastern distribution center of the Sony Corporation in Atlanta to buy these special small tape recorders, and they cost more than $300 each!

Mercer is a very caring school, which understands the handicapped. It was good to get my higher education there.

## Chapter 36

# *My Sea Voyage*

On December 3, 1983, my daddy, my mother, and I met my sister Beverly at the Atlanta airport. It was a cold and rainy day that Saturday morning at 8:00 a.m. We had to fly to Miami to start our sea voyage.

When we got to the Miami airport, we caught a bus that took us to the docks of the huge *S.S. Norway*. This was the largest cruise ship in the world at that time. It is 1,035 feet, more than three football fields, in length. If the *Norway* were placed in an upright position, it would be almost as tall as the Empire State Building.

The *Norway* is like a city out on the open sea. It has everything any town has, plus such things as a closed circuit TV station, a hospital, a Las Vegas-style revue called "Sea Legs," a gambling room where I won three dollars from a quarter slot machine, and many other activities.

The Norway had two dining rooms, to serve 2,400 passengers. We had the early seating in the Windward Dining Room, with a man and lady from Sacramento, California, at our table. Roger was in the construction business, and his friend Leslie worked with him. We had a great waiter named Victor. He did a lot of things for me, such as putting my napkin in my lap, cutting up my meat, and reading my mind and bringing me a glass of tea. The last night all of the waiters did a parade and dance with trays of flaming baked Alaska on their heads.

The activities on the *S.S. Norway* for a week were the main things we did on the cruise. The ship was so smooth that we hardly knew we were sailing. We went to St. Thomas, Nassau in the Bahamas, and to an out-island owned by the Norwegian Caribbean Line. When we got to St. Thomas, the temperature was higher than ninety degrees that day. It was so hot my mother nearly fainted. We all had to get back to the ship by 3:00 p.m. Since the *Norway* is so big, it cannot dock at any of the Caribbean Islands we visited, so everyone had to use 500-passenger tenders to go ashore and to return to the ship. The dock in Miami was the only dock on our itinerary that could hold the Norway.

Every night on the ship there was some big entertainment. Nightly events included the captain's cocktail party, a fair night on the deck, the Broadway play *My Fair Lady*, and the group called "Sea Legs" put on a great show.

The most meaningful thing that happened to me on the *Norway* was meeting the famous piano player Roger Williams, who was the main featured entertainer. Before his concert, he spotted me walking down the aisle, left the stage, and came and shook my hand! I felt honored that a great entertainer like Roger Williams took the time to come over to talk to me. He impressed me so much that I attended both his shows, where he would smile at us and make personal remarks to us, as we sat on the front row.

The next day Daddy and I went to a video interview that Williams was on. The cruise director talked with him for a few minutes and then asked for questions from the audience.

I asked him, "How many records did you make?"

His answer was, "Eighty albums."

Roger Williams started playing the piano when he was only three years old. He went on to get a degree in engineering, but stayed with music education, and later got his degree and then a Ph.D. in Music.

On the last night of the cruise, after dinner, Daddy and I met a nice gentleman and chatted with him.

After a few minutes of small talk, Daddy asked him, "Where are you flying back to tomorrow?"

The man replied, "California."

After we left him, we realized that we had been talking to the big movie star Ernest Borgnine, who had been as friendly as any ordinary person!

It was easy to get lost on the *S.S. Norway*. When we went to see *My Fair Lady*, Daddy and I were upstairs while mother was downstairs looking for us. We did not know the theater had entrances to it on two different levels.

I liked St. Thomas better than the Bahamas. St. Thomas is mainly a ridge of mountainous hills running east and west, and has little tillable land. We rode up to the Mountain Top Restaurant and had a banana daiquiri, its specialty. The Atlantic Ocean is on one side of this island and the Caribbean Sea is on the other. The view of both is beautiful and spectacular from the Mountain Top Restaurant. The water is clear and many different shades of blue. Nearly everything I saw in St. Thomas was delightful. I especially liked Bluebeard's Castle, which was very interesting, and I enjoyed walking around it.

When we got to Nassau, I spent most of my time looking for a woven straw basket for my girlfriend Tracy. But all the vendors tried to sell me a hat with my name on it. I did not like for them to grab me by the arm and beg for my business. But I did finally find a nice basket and bought it.

The best stop on the cruise was the out-island. It was a day of sunbathing, watching volleyball, and listening to the calypso band. The other side of the out-island was reserved for passengers who went nude, but I did not go and look! Beverly took part in the *Norway*'s "Dive-In" program, which taught everyone how to snorkel.

It was a wonderful cruise. I had the best time of my life. However, we were unlucky coming back home. When we got to the Miami docks, everybody's suitcases were under one leaky roof in a heavy rain. All passengers waited on the *Norway* while the ship was being unloaded and the baggage was checked by the U.S. Customs Service. It was a madhouse, with 2,400 passengers all trying to get their belongings at the same time.

We arrived at the Atlanta airport safely, but our baggage went to Dayton, Ohio. However, Delta delivered all of our things within twenty-four hours to our home in Macon, so everything turned out all right.

## Chapter 37

# *My Periods of Depression*

All my life I have been a happy person, joyful and optimistic. But that all drastically changed in the Spring of 1983, when I was well on my way toward getting through college.

In late March, at the beginning of the third quarter, I began to feel terrible. I became afraid of everything, agitated, depressed, and felt worthless. Nothing like that had ever happened to me before. I did not know what was happening to me. My parents tried to encourage and help me, but I continued to feel very bad.

Some of my discouragement may have had to do with changing my major so much. As already stated, I started off at Mercer majoring in Christianity. But after a good many lectures to students, and with the encouragement of my advisors, I had changed my major to Education. At that time I had already completed some general education requirements and religious courses. Then, in about November of 1982 I had decided to make my major Special Education. I felt I could do a better job in the field of Special Education than most, since I had been a student in Special Education at T. D. Tinsley School for eleven years. I also thought, being handicapped myself, I would have an advantage in this work.

But after then taking many Education courses, I changed my mind. I thought four or five years training for this would be too long. So about April first I went to the registrar's office to talk about possibly changing my major again, and they assigned me a new advisor. This advisor had taught me Introduction to Exceptional Children, and I had done well in the course. He met with me and made a list of the Special Education courses I would need to take yet to get a degree in that major. I would have to take fourteen to sixteen more required courses! And a lot of courses I had completed would not count toward this major. That was awful news, as, to continue in this field, it would take several years longer than the five or six years I had already expected it would take me to graduate.

For the next couple of weeks in April, although anxious and depressed, I continued to try to muddle through school, going to classes, but not really accomplishing anything.

Then, to make matters worse, still in that bad April, most of my Education professors at Mercer called for and had a conference with my parents, primarily discussing how I would function teaching a Special Education class, with my speech impediment. I was not allowed at the meeting. The conclusion was that it would be a long and hard road for me, and that it would be difficult for me to get a job because of my speech.

When my parents told me about what was said at this conference, I got even more depressed about my future plans—so upset that I wanted to drop out of Mercer entirely. I had not been doing well in either of my two courses, English Poetry and Math for Teachers. Both of these were very hard subjects.

My mind began to form ideas like: "I'm just no good. I do not need a college degree. I could just get a job right now."

When I told my folks I wanted to drop out of Mercer they were extremely upset and sad. They pointed out that they thought such action would be a big mistake, since I had worked so hard, and was well over halfway through. They were concerned, and tried to help me every way they could.

So I continued trying to make it. But one night was the most terrible I have ever had. I stayed agitated and shaky all night, had wild thoughts, and even thought about harming myself. The next morning I called my folks to come to the dormitory and get me and take me home. I was supposed to have a poetry test that day, but there was no way I could have taken it in my condition. Mother and Daddy came to the school and picked me up.

I remained in bad shape, so my parents took me to an emergency session with a psychologist, Dr. N. Archer Moore. He gave me some good advice, and suggested that I drop one of my two courses, to see how that would work out, but he warned that it might be necessary for me to quit school entirely, if my agitation did not improve.

For a week or so I seemed to be maybe doing a little better. But then I again became wild, agitated, crying, unable to sleep, and unable to do anything constructive. My parents took me as an emergency to see Dr. Ray McCard, a psychiatrist friend of my father's. Dr. McCard recommended that I completely drop out of Mercer, and he put me on a mild antidepressant drug. Fortunately, that was the last day of the third quarter that a student could drop courses without getting a flunking grade. Therefore I got two WIs (withdrawals incomplete) rather than two WFs (withdrawals failing). Mercer officials expressed sorrow at my decision, but said they would be happy to let me start back at any time, if I changed my mind, and that my two WIs would not be harmful to my returning and would not affect my grade average.

Shortly after dropping out, and having no responsibility to study or to make big education decisions, my attitude and morale improved. My agitation went away, and I no longer needed medication. But I stayed a little depressed.

About a week or two after I dropped out, Tracy Jones, my good friend, called me one Saturday morning from Augusta, where she was in nursing school. From the tone of my voice she immediately knew something was badly wrong with me. She realized I needed somebody to talk to, so that same afternoon she drove to Macon to see me.

Tracy gave me some good advice, and said, "You came this far at Mercer, why stop now? You need a college education, and what good will it be if you never finish?"

Tracy really gave me a good pep talk and lifted my spirits about finishing Mercer.

I also discussed my depression with my minister, and with a few other professionals. The one who helped me the most was David Drake, a professional counselor, and the husband of one of my Human Services professors, Dr. Mary Ann Drake. David seemed to understand me very well and he was a good listener when I talked about my feelings. When he could not understand my speech, I would write the sentence out on a piece of paper so he could read it. But he usually understood me very well. I had weekly counseling with him for a long time.

That summer I realized that my dropping out of Mercer had been a terribly bad mistake. My parents and I decided the best thing to do probably would be for me to go back to Mercer in the fall, and to work toward getting an Individualized Major. The purpose of an Individualized Major is to tailor the requirements to the needs of the student and the school. This major has very strict requirements, must be approved by a faculty board, and is seldom given.

So that summer I talked to Dr. Thomas Glennon, the head of the Psychology Department, and he was still considered my main advisor. When I told him I wanted to return to Mercer in the fall, but that I might want to change to an Individualized Major, he pointed out that a lot of the courses I had already taken, and more that I wanted to take, would give me credit toward a degree in Human Services. I liked what Tom told me about this major, because it has to do with helping people. All my life, meeting and helping people has been greatly important to me. I would much rather be working and aiding others than to be alone.

So I returned to Mercer the next September, went back into the dormitory, and had no trouble that year, either with my studies or with depression. I took a Human Services course every quarter. These Human Services courses were always interesting to me, and I made mostly A's and B's in them.

During the junior year this major required the student, in addition to his academic studies, to perform an internship in the field of human services. My internship that year was at the United Cerebral Palsy Center in Macon. I helped the teachers and therapists, worked in the office, and tried to help with the handicapped children.

In the summer of 1984, just before my last year at Mercer, I got somewhat agitated, upset, and depressed again. But my spirits were greatly boosted from two events. First, I received word that my application for my senior year's Mercer Human Services internship at Charter Lake Psychiatric Hospital had been accepted. I had been worried about this, as appropriate internships in the human services field in Macon were hard to get, yet this was required for my degree. Secondly, my great friend and former K.A. Little Brother Mark Brittain came to Macon and visited me. After that, I felt good, and I am thankful that I have never had that awful depression and agitation again.

As mentioned, changing majors several times, making additional courses required and some I had already taken noncrediting, and that bad conference the Special Education professors had with my parents, might have had something to do with my first episode of depression, when I dropped out of Mercer. Then, not knowing until the last minute whether I could get a good internship my senior year may have helped cause me to feel bad that summer.

But another factor may have been important, too. You will recall in my chapter on "The Brain Pacemaker" that this equipment had to be turned off in November 1984, when we found out the wires were broken. There is no way we can know how long before this the pacemaker had not been working right. It could have been for a year or two. All of my emotional problems were in the period of about a year and a half before the instrument was cut off. My doctor father feels that this improperly functioning pacemaker may have been the main or only cause of my agitation and depression. We will never know.

## Chapter 38

# *Last Year in College*

As mentioned, my application for an internship for my senior year was finally accepted, but it had not been easy to find or to get. During the summer of 1984 one of my advisors at Mercer, Mary Jane Pollitzer, and I had started looking around for a place where I could do my Human Services internship. Human Services, my major, is very similar to Psychology or Sociology. One of the last requirements of the major is to work in a healthcare setting fifteen to twenty hours per week. Mary Jane made appointments and took me to several places for interviews.

The place we liked best for my internship was Charter Lake Psychiatric Hospital. We talked to the head teacher, Ron Southerland. He said he would like for me to work on the adolescent floor there, using the computer, but that he would have to get permission from the hospital administrator first. Ron said I should hear about this in about a couple of weeks.

In a few weeks I was notified that the administrator had approved my application for internship.

So I went to Charter Lake Hospital. At first Ron said he wanted me to work on the computer, but that turned out not to be a good idea, because the patients would stop their work to see what I was doing. Most of the teenage patients at Charter Lake were in junior or senior high school, so the hospital had a school on the adolescent unit. There was a teacher who worked with Ron and me. If a teenager needed some help in a particular subject, the teacher would help that student. Otherwise, the students worked on their own.

After I had been working at the hospital for three or four weeks, Ron gave me two duties. They were to keep "Goal Sheets" and "Therapeutic

Trial Visits," or TTVs for short. Goal sheets had all of the problems for each patient, and they would write beside each item how they were doing on each problem. These young people had problems like suicidal ideation, poor self-esteem, family conflict, depression, or drug withdrawal.

Ron wanted the teenagers to write out in detail about the problems they were having, and how they were working on them. My duty was to make sure the patients filled out these Goal Sheets thoroughly and correctly. They had to write a lot more than just "Still a problem" or "Working on it."

My other main duty was to help these youngsters fill out their TTV sheets. Every Saturday morning half of the teenagers went home. On the TTV sheets the patients had to write down when they would be picked up, who would be responsible for them while they were away from Charter Lake, what they wanted to accomplish during the weekend, and what time they would return to the hospital. The main purpose of the TTV sheets was to see if the adolescents were ready to go ahead with their everyday lives, before they were discharged from the hospital. Many of them required a lot of help from me with this paperwork.

It was hard for me to see teenagers having so much trouble in their lives, especially those whose families rejected them, as I had had a happy childhood and a very close family. I felt sorry for the adolescents at the hospital there and wished I could make everything all right for them. I enjoyed my eight months working at Charter Lake, and it was a rewarding experience for me.

It was nice to see two of my friends working there. Henry Thomas was a Methodist minister who worked in the office typing up records on patients. I really admired Henry for coming out of retirement and going to work for the hospital. Another of my friends was one of the former Kappa Alpha Roses named Patrice. She was in a lot of Human Services courses with me. Patrice and I had decided that being education majors was totally wrong for us, so we had both changed to Human Services. That move was the best decision that I ever made at Mercer.

A lot of people helped me with all of the Human Services requirements, but one of the best tutors that I had was Joanne Williams. She helped me for five quarters with papers and with homework assignments.

When I got upset or worried, Joanne would always cheer me up. We became very close friends, and Joanne was my Old South date that year. Joanne helped me through some hard times in my college career. Besides being my great tutor, we had some fun, too, by going to movies, out to dinner, out to the Macon Mall, and going to my church.

My two Human Services professors were very good to me. The funniest professor at Mercer was the chairman of that department, Dr. Tom Glennon. I had him for three Human Services courses and a Psychology class. He was always a cutup, saying that I got drunk every night—which was not true. In spite of all this, Tom had the reputation of being a good teacher and a fun guy to be around.

Dr. Mary Ann Drake was in charge of my internship, and I had class with her on Monday afternoons. The class had about twenty-five students working in different health settings. Some of the places classmates worked in were nursing homes, hospitals, and welfare offices, and they also helped out with needy families. All of the interns would meet at 3:00 p.m. every Monday to talk about the people they were working with, or to hear guest speakers. I had a man to come from Charter Lake and talk about working with troubled adolescents.

Also we wrote up case studies to share with the group. The class enjoyed the two case studies that I wrote about, and hearing about the patients with whom I worked. Because of confidentiality, I used false patient names in both papers. The thing that I liked most about the Human Services Department was that all of the professors and students were on a first-name basis.

At about this time I got another fine K.A. "Little Brother." His name was James Sheffield. Even though he was my little brother for only about a year, he was a good friend then, and remains one now. He has visited in my home many times. My father wrote recommendations for him for medical schools, and after a long and hard undergraduate journey in several places—and sometimes being out of school entirely—he finally got his wish and was accepted to a medical school, and he has now received his M.D. degree.

It was spring quarter of my senior year and I was excited about my soon-to-come graduation from Mercer University. My college career took me two years longer than standard because I changed my major two times. Also I only took ten hours or two courses per quarter, instead of the usual three courses and fifteen hours, but I made up a lot of this by going to summer sessions almost every summer.

I was very honored that the K.A.s presented me with the Hentz Houser Award for being the most outstanding graduating senior brother. The recipient is voted on by the brothers of Kappa Alpha and announced each spring just before the Old South Ball. When they called my name I was overjoyed and appreciative of this wonderful honor and recognition. A large walnut plaque with brass nameplates hangs in the Gold Room of the K.A. house. Each year the name of the brother receiving this award is engraved on a new plate. The plate for 1985 is inscribed with my name.

My feelings about leaving Mercer and all of my friends were very mixed. I started wondering about my future. Daddy and I began going around on Thursday afternoons, talking to people about a job for me after graduation. Thursday afternoon was the only time my father was not working in his office or the hospital, so that was the best time for us to go job hunting. However, I did not find work right away.

The day of my college graduation finally came. It was wonderful to see my good friend and my first K.A. Little Brother Mark Brittain there for the biggest event of my life. All of my family ate lunch together at the K.A. table in the Mercer dining room before time for the ceremony at 3:00 p.m.

I sat on the front row in cap and gown, this time in black (in contrast to the white at my high school graduation) in a chair on the front row on the right, while all 500 candidates marched into the Macon Coliseum. To my surprise, when President Godsey called my name to receive my diploma, the entire student body, the faculty, and then the whole Coliseum audience rose and gave me a standing ovation! I had received a similar ovation at my high school graduation, but this was better, with more people present, and the response was louder and with more enthusiasm. I was shocked, speechless and very happy at the same moment. It was hard to hear anything because of all of the applause. I felt very honored that the student body, faculty, and the audience had cheered me so. It was as if I had been a hero in Vietnam or had taken part in something wonderful. There were many special people there to see me graduate. In all, about sixty members of my family, friends, and former teachers came and sat together in the same section.

A few days before the graduation, my mother had invited a lot of my relatives and some friends to come over to our house after the ceremony, to celebrate with some champagne. We had thought about thirty-five people would show up, but we invited a number of former teachers and old friends as we saw them at the Coliseum. Altogether, about a hundred people came to our house to my graduation party. Some made speeches and toasts. Four of my young lady cousins sang and danced to a cute song they had rehearsed for this special occasion, and they presented it with much humor, and with high leg kicks.

The song was to the tune of "Hernando's Hideaway," but they had made up new words for this occasion.

*Gary, we're here to honor you,*
*And tell you that we love you too,*
*For you have really met the test,*
*And measured way above the rest—the best.*

*Your patience with your fellow man,*
*Your willingness to say, "I can,"*
*The way you do the things you do,*
*Have been an inspiration, too—so true.*

*Your faith, your love, your friendly smile,*
*Exhibit total lack of guile.*
*The warmth and strength that you portray,*
*Lighten up and brighten every day—Ole!*

Everybody was keyed up and excited and happy. We all had such a good time that the party lasted really late, but it was such a memorable event for me that I hated to see the evening come to an end.

Many things about that evening were emotional for me, but one thing especially touched my heart. My sister Beverly, of course, had come down for the ceremony and party. Accompanying her was her friend and pastor, a Marietta Methodist minister named Rev. David Bowen. I found out that this Sunday morning at his church, before driving down to Macon to see me graduate, he had made me the subject of his sermon. He told his audience about how tough it had been for me to get a good education, and about how fortunate I was that I had been able to get transferred from special to regular education, due to the untiring efforts of so many people, especially my parents. Rev. Bowen gave me a tape of this sermon, and every time I hear this tribute it gives me a special feeling about my life.

My favorite part of this tape is where David says:

> Gary, you may not speak like a Philadelphia attorney pleading a case, your words may not be formed perfectly, and it may take you a long time to get the sentence out—you are going to get the sentence out—but it sometimes is an agonizing process unless you are loved by the people who listen.

For a graduation present, my parents took me, along with two cousins, Jane and Kim McKissack, to Acapulco, Mexico, for five days. We stayed at the beautiful Acapulco Princess Hotel, where Howard Hughes had become fatally ill, and where scenes for the TV show "Dynasty" were filmed for several episodes. The Princess has waterfalls, lakes, pools, nine restaurants, and an open lobby that always has a cool breeze blowing through it. We all fell in love with their mai tais, a drink with tropical juices and rum. One day we rented a Jeep and drove across the mountain to Acapulco Bay to see the famous cliff divers. I do not see how they can jump from so high and live. My Acapulco vacation was a good trip and my parents were great to take me.

## Chapter 39

# *Five Days of Partying*

On May 20, 1987, my mother, my father and I met my brother David at the Satellite Airport parking lot in Atlanta. We got on a van that took us to the Eastern baggage check-in. The reason for our trip to Buffalo, New York, was to go to the wedding of my other brother Clark. Buffalo is the home of buffalo wings and the Buffalo Bills football team.

When we got to the loading gate, passengers were boarding the plane. Unknown to us, the plane's departure time had been run up ten minutes. By the time we got there the plane was already fully loaded, except for four seats in the first class section. So we got to ride in first class without paying extra. The stewardess gave us a drink before we left the ground, then, as soon as we were in the air, came right away with our lunch. The smooth flight took a little less than two hours. First class is the way to go!

When the plane landed in Buffalo, the bride-to-be, Tina, and her parents, Wilbur and Phyllis Jost, met us at the gate. Daddy rented a four-door, navy-blue car from Avis. Tina rode in our car, to show us where our hotel was located, which was about twenty miles from the airport.

The hotel was large and nice, although not real fancy, and it had clean, roomy, and quiet rooms. My daddy reserved about eighteen rooms on the second floor for all of our family, relatives, and friends who were coming for Clark and Tina's big event. My parents had a nice suite on the main floor. This hotel was the best place for us to stay, because it was fairly close to the events of the wedding—and its night club, gift shop, and restaurant were fine places to gather.

About two hours after we arrived, Tina and her father took us to an Italian restaurant where we ate dinner. After dinner all of us went to the harness racing track to watch Tina's brother-in-law drive his two-wheeled cart in the eighth horse race. It was interesting to see how big horse racing is in New York. Some people looked as if they stayed at the tracks all day long betting large amounts of money. I lost two dollars.

The next day we went back to the airport to meet my Uncle Joe, Aunt Mary Helen, and cousins Bonnylin, Bennett, and Cathy. Also arriving was a friend of our family, Patsy Fried. Uncle Joe rented a car, and he gave Daddy a hard time because he got his auto cheaper. I rode with Tina, who led the way back to the hotel for the newcomers. From Atlanta Aunt Lil and Uncle Jack flew up, as did Uncle Harold and Aunt Betty from Virginia. Julie and David Bowman flew in from Atlanta. Also their son David, Jr., his wife Dena, and their children came from Amherst, New York. That night we all went for a great seafood dinner at a restaurant in a nearby town.

The following morning just my family went into the big city. Buffalo formerly was known for its industries, but had suffered from a deflated economy in recent years. It was sad to see so many factories closed down. There were many "Archie Bunker" looking houses en route.

We saw many interesting things before heading back to the airport, for the last time before the wedding, to pick up my sister Beverly and her son Daniel. It was especially thrilling to greet Beverly and Daniel, because they had come all the way from Aspen, Colorado, where they had moved to from Atlanta just two months earlier. They looked wonderful.

That night all of the wedding party and guests except Clark and Tina went twenty-five miles for dinner at a lodge overlooking beautiful Lake Erie. I was surprised to learn that in the winter the lake is frozen over enough so that people can walk and ice skate on it. That was hard for me to imagine, doing such a thing. It was good to get together and spend time visiting with all of my relatives and Mr. and Mrs. Jost.

A cousin brought his video camera. Mike and Bonnylin filmed us starting out from the hotel, in the car on the way, and as we were walking into the restaurant. Later we enjoyed and laughed at the tapes.

Everybody woke up early the next morning to drive about thirty miles to Niagara Falls. Pasty was in our car and took over as the navigator. There were almost no highway signs to guide us, but there was one little one about the size of an envelope, which was the only one in that area to guide all the many tourists. Everybody had told us to drive on the Canadian side because it is much prettier than the American side. So we went that way, and it was beautiful.

When we got to the falls we went down long steps to a boat called "Maid of the Mist." They gave each passenger a bright blue raincoat with hood to wear. We looked like Martians! The boat took us right under the falls. The ride was very wet, and the falls are really one of the seven wonders of the world.

From a high-up eating place where we had lunch, we got a spectacular view of both the American and Canadian falls. I will always remember that sight. All the grounds on the Canadian side anywhere near the town or falls were very well kept. Gardens of flowers were everywhere. Mother especially liked the "manicured look" of the yards. We read in a newspaper a few days later that a man had fatally jumped from the falls about an hour or two after we left.

That night we went to the rehearsal at the church, and the rehearsal dinner afterwards. The wedding was to be at a United Methodist Church in a nearby town, about twenty miles from our hotel, so that is where we rehearsed. The church, which was built in 1819, was in the little community of Eden, New York. It had stained glass windows and about twenty-two pews, and was a very beautiful setting for a wedding. After practicing at the church, all of the wedding party met with guests at Lakeview resort for the rehearsal dinner.

After we feasted on a good meal, all of my family and guests gave Clark and Tina many champagne toasts.

Since Clark loves to fish, the last thing that I said in my speech was, "Clark, I hope you will spend more time with your new bride than with the fishes."

While I still had the floor, I also said, "I have learned a lot of things from my brother, even how to lose some of my hair!"

When all of the toasts were made, a disc jockey came in and played all kinds of music.

The day of the wedding was very busy. My daddy was Clark's best man. David was an usher, Beverly was a bridesmaid, and I was a groomsman. The other attendants were Tina's sister Ruth as matron of honor; Tina's friend Karen, a bridesmaid; and Roger Knight, Clark and Tina's Orlando friend, an usher. Tina's niece Crystal was junior bridesmaid; her little nephew Stuart was ringbearer; and the flower girl was Jill Thompson.

I went to the church with Clark and Daddy two hours before the wedding, to get ready for the event. It was a very lovely ceremony, with about seventy-five people in the congregation. Tina wore a gorgeous satin wedding dress with a long train. I wore a light gray-blue tux that was modelled after those in the "Dynasty" television show. It made me feel like a million!

After the ceremony all of us went to the reception at Shoreline Manor. We stood in the receiving line to greet all of the many guests. Then we ate dinner at the head table. The wedding reception was managed by the same man who had put on our rehearsal dinner at Lakeview. There were four special dances: Clark and Tina; Clark and his mother; Tina and her father; and then all the rest of the wedding party. It was a lot of fun dancing with everybody. The music again was very good. Unlike in the South, the reception party lasted four hours.

The next day was Memorial Day and our trip was coming to an end. Mike and Bonnylin and many others took an early flight home. Roger drove Beverly and Daniel to their gate, which was at the opposite end of the airport. It was sad to see them leave for Colorado, because we would not get to see them often.

Clark and Tina's wedding was much fun, but I was glad to get back home and relax. After the honeymoon the bride and groom happily settled down in their condo in Orlando, and had fun riding in Clark's Corvette.

Later they moved from the condo to a large, white, two-story home. They also had a baby girl, Christy, who is now six years old. Unfortunately, the marriage broke up, and Clark and Tina are divorced.

## Chapter 40

# *Fun the Mexican Way*

At 4:08 a.m. on June 18, 1989, the Youth Choir of Riverside United Methodist Church left for Hartsfield International Airport in Atlanta. It was too early for the average person, but it was not for twenty-five youth and seven adult counselors, who were to fly to Cancún, Mexico, for four days in the sun. Our flight on Key Air was smooth, and took two hours and fifteen minutes.

It was so hot and humid in Cancún that the group and I had trouble getting used to it at first. Everybody went through customs without any trouble except for Todd, Damon, and Flynn. Customs would not allow Todd's amplifier into Mexico without proof of ownership. They finally straightened things out and got through customs after about two hours.

Meanwhile the rest of the group checked in at our hotel, the Aquamarina. We had rooms on all six floors! About fifteen minutes after we checked in, people from our host church came to get us for their worship service. The church was in one room above a store, and with no air conditioning, and with only two big floor fans. The temperature in this room must have been ninety to one hundred degrees. It was so hot I almost fell asleep. In order to get to the church room, we had had to climb three flights of steps with no handrail. It was a bit scary being in that narrow stairwell! The church service was very difficult to follow because it was in Spanish.

Back at the hotel, I ate lunch with some of the youth and counselors at the snack bar by the pool. After a good meal we all went sunbathing. I wore my white and blue cap in order to keep the sun off my forehead. The pool was great because it had two sections. As I do not swim, I liked the wading pool best. It allowed me to float on my back and to walk in the water all by myself.

That night the choir put on its first concert, which was held on the patio of the hotel, and it was good. I was the only non-singing counselor on the trip. After the concert the hotel fed us a real Mexican dinner. It was wonderful, but unusual! Right after we finished eating everybody went to his hotel room to get some sleep, after the long, eighteen-hour activities of the first day.

My roommate was the choir director Jim Barrow. In the room next to ours were two crazy guys, Tommy and Harry. It was not too long before these guys found the nearest Domino's pizza. Everybody on the trip had brought his own breakfast food, to cut down on expenses. I took apple juice, Hi-C punch, nuts, granola bars, and yogurt peanuts. Jim and I were in the room the refrigerator was in, which was convenient for me. On each of the four days somebody new was assigned to help me around. The first day Jim pushed me around in a wheelchair and helped me with my food tray. On the second day it was Damon and Jody Riggs's day to be my escorts.

Everybody wanted to go to downtown Cancún to shop at a big market, which we did. I bought a handsome brown leather belt for myself, and a pretty bracelet for my mother. The most exciting thing about the market was that you could talk the merchants down to a low price. My belt was marked thirty-five dollars but I got it for about eighteen! Some of the other youth made good deals too.

That night we were to sing in a small room at the Crystal Palace Hotel, where John Forsythe had hosted the Miss Universe contest a week or two before. Unfortunately, we were unable to go into the room where Miss Universe had been held. And we were about an hour late getting started, due to slow service for supper at a Mexican restaurant about ten miles away from the Crystal Palace. However, a small group of people had waited there to hear us. When we did put on the concert, the audience was enthusiastic and enjoyed it. It was fun being in such a beautiful place.

On the third day of our journey it was time to relax. I mostly laid around the pool or went to the beach all morning. Something unusual I did with Flynn and Damon was to walk about 250 feet out into the ocean to an old abandoned pier. All the way out there the water was warm, and was never more than waist deep. Some of the group wanted to do some more serious wave jumping at another beach, which had bigger waves. So a lot of us wandered to the Sheraton Hotel, which was about ten miles from our hotel. I had never jumped waves so high as I did at the Sheraton beach. There were big whoppers! Some of them were over my head. However, we had a good time in that rough water.

Then it was time to go back to the Aquamarina, to get ready for our last concert. For our last performance, we sang outside on the square in downtown Cancún. The choir had only sung three or four songs when it started raining. All of us then went and sat in the bus, and the Cancún preacher prayed it would stop raining. After fifteen minutes the rain did stop, and we started the concert over, to the biggest audience yet! When the concert was over, we took the Cancún church people out to eat at Denny's. A lot of the youth, along with myself, ordered a good American hamburger.

Wednesday was our last full day in Mexico. Except for Damon and Jody, we all rode on a bus for four hours to the famous Mexican ruins. We stopped half way there in order to buy a cold drink and relax for a few minutes. I noticed from my window that the natives lived in grass huts. Our tour guide said they thought they were living in nice houses, because the natives did not know how well we lived in America.

When we finally got to the pyramids it was time for our group to eat lunch, which was provided by the tour. It was a good dinner of Mexican dishes. Our guide told Gail Pollock and me to go at our own speed. Gail is the director of music at Riverside, and she did a wonderful job of planning and leading our Cancún trip. Both of us had a good time going on our own. Gail made a big deal of my climbing a pyramid on my own, and she took a picture of me on top of it.

It was very refreshing to get a free Coke while returning by bus to our hotel. The bus stopped at a gift shop en route and I purchased a letter opener for my daddy. I was glad to get back to the Aquamarina by 7:00 p.m.

The departure day of our trip was very disorderly. Gail said that everybody must be in the lobby at ten minutes after 10:00 a.m. to catch the bus to go to the airport. While I was hurriedly packing, somebody called to let us know our flight would be two hours late. So I decided to go to the pool one last time. Now the bus was supposed to pick us up at 12:30, and our flight was at 3:30 p.m. When we finally got to the Cancún airport, our flight was leaving in about fifteen minutes! The Lord must have been with all of us in order to find time for everyone to pay his ten dollars to get out of Mexico.

When the plane finally landed in Atlanta, Jim and I had to wait a long time for the airport attendants to bring me a wheelchair. I had Jim take me to the bank in the airport to get my money changed back to American currency. It was great to be back in Georgia and to see our drivers—Bobby George, John Irwin, and Jim Pollock, who were at the airport waiting for us. What a wonderful trip! How great to be home!

The Cancún trip was a rewarding experience for everybody. Shortly after getting home we raised money for an air conditioner for the Cancún church. This we did by appealing for donations from our Riverside Church families. They responded willingly. Now the Mexican people will not have to suffer from the heat as they worship in their Cancún Methodist church. What a Christian feeling this gives each of us who went on this trip!

## Chapter 41

# *Life after Mercer*

In the summer of 1985 I had graduated from Mercer and had returned to Macon from a trip to Acapulco. Now I felt I could give more time toward helping my church. All my life I have felt strongly that I should go to Sunday School and church every week. I told the youth director then, Rev. John Irwin, that I would like to be a youth counsclor, and he made me one. John and I worked together with the young people at Riverside United Methodist Church, and became great friends. We had many conversations, often eating together, and over the phone, about ways to help the youth. Some were from broken homes or had emotional problems. I think the reason I wanted to be a counselor was to try to help them find God during this difficult period in their lives. When I was a teenager in this same youth group it had been the most meaningful time in my life.

As a counselor I accompanied the youth on many good trips. One great trip, that we went on every year, was a skiing trip to Sugar Mountain, North Carolina. It is always fun watching the youth have such a good time on the slopes, and in just being part of the fellowship, although I do not ski.

Another good trip was in the summer of 1988, when I went with the youth to Washington, D.C. We all had our pictures taken on the steps of the Capitol with our representative, J. Roy Rowland. We had many other enjoyable trips, also, as well as having a lot of fun and strengthening of our religious faith at home in Macon.

Working with the youth was rewarding, but ordinarily took only several hours a week. What I really wanted and needed was a full-time paying job. Jobs are difficult to find in Macon, and having a speech impediment and slow typing due to cerebral palsy in my hands makes it twice as hard for me to find meaningful work.

My oldest brother David had the good idea for me to try to find some volunteer work, that doing volunteer work was better than doing nothing, and that sometimes doing that can help lead to a paying job. David called Volunteer Macon. The lady there said Georgia Legal Services needed someone to do volunteer computer work. I went to see them, and we agreed I would go there three afternoons a week, typing legal data into the computer. But, after I started going there, about half the time the computer would be out of order, and there would be nothing else for me to do. I felt it was inconsiderate for them not to call me at home when the computer was not working, before letting my mother drive me to this office for nothing. Also I felt they should have had some other tasks for me to do when the computer was down. However, the people were very friendly, and it was interesting to learn something about the law. I worked there for about six months.

All the time I was doing this volunteer work my father and I were going to many places looking for a paying job for me, preferably full-time. We made lists, called people on the phone, and talked to friends. But the main thing we did was to "hit the streets." Some days we went to fifteen different offices.

Finally I found employment with the Bibb County Department of Family and Children Services, called DFACS for short. My main duty there was to tend to the outgoing mail. The mailroom was on the first floor. My boss would give me a big Wendy's bag to take up to the second floor to put all the mail in. I would have to get out 300 to 600 pieces of mail daily, metering each item, but someone else would come about 2:30 p.m. to help. Until then I would be the only one in the office handling this responsibility.

Many of the workers here were in the bad habit of waiting until the last moment in the afternoon before getting their outgoing mail to me. So about 3:00 p.m. we would have to lock the door to prevent this, in order to get all the mail we already had ready for the postman, who picked it up at 4:00 p.m. DFACS arranged for its driver to take me to and from work every day, and I thought this was very nice of them.

After about seven months of working here my job ended abruptly due to lack of funds. The director said I had been performing well, but that my position had been cut. I was very sad about this, because I had made some good friends there, and I was making money, which gave me a sense of independence.

For six months my father and I went everywhere looking for work for me. We went to new places, as well as back to old places we thought were good bets.

Many of the bosses would say, “We wish we could help you, but we don’t have the funds to hire anybody.”

I got tired of hearing that. I felt many of them would tell you anything just to get you out of their offices. But I am sure some of them would have hired me if they had had the money to do so. My ideal job would be one where I could work without the fear of losing my position due to lack of funds. Of course, I would not turn down any offer, even if the work were temporary.

In the summer of 1987 I did find a federal government job. I became a Program Clerk, GS-4, at the V.A. Hospital in Dublin, fifty-five miles from my house. My father was a physician on the staff there. It was hard getting up at 5:30 a.m. every day in order to be ready to leave by 7:00. I would ride in the car with my father or with another Macon doctor who commuted there.

This V.A. center had just received a big computer. My instructions were to make the initial typing of the names of all the 1,000 employees, plus much other information, mostly in number codes, into the core memory of the computer, for a permanent file. This was very important and exacting work, which took me about six weeks to complete. My boss complimented me on my accuracy, which he said was much more important than speed in this job. It was good to get this praise, but it was even better to get the good money this job paid. I am sure the V.A. center there is still using some of this information I put in.

Unfortunately, this employment was only temporary, for ninety days. At the end of this three-month period all 300 temporary employees, including me, were let go, due to lack of funds. I felt it was unfair that I had been laid off my first two paying jobs for that reason. Losing this job, although I had known it was classified as temporary, was depressing and hard for me to deal with. I felt sorry for the other temporary workers who, like me, had been let go, especially for a divorced lady in my office who had two small children.

So again I was out of work, through no fault of my own. I felt this was not right. My father and I began again the huge task of updating job lists, going back to people who had seemed interested in helping me before, and in going to new places and contacting new people. I did most of the talking during these interviews, but my father was with me, in case some person could not understand me. But most of the time the potential employer and I had no trouble communicating.

Then again opportunity knocked, with a tip coming from my good friend and computer expert and teacher, Dr. Barbara Clinton. She had previously given me some private computer lessons. Barbara said a friend of hers, who was the principal of Joseph Clisby Magnet School in Macon, had some computer work she needed someone to do. I went there and was immediately hired. I was told to put all the students' and teachers' names, addresses, zip codes, phone numbers, student grades, and other information into the school's new computer. Although this was a nonpaying, volunteer, part-time job, it was good experience, and I got my foot in the door of the Bibb County Board of Education. On the completion of this work the Clisby principal wrote a good letter of recommendation for me to the School Board. This helped me get my next job.

A few months later, on the same day, I got two job offers! The first was for part-time employment doing computer work for the Georgia Power Company. The other was to work in the Bibb County Board of Education Warehouse. I took the latter offer, because it was full-time.

My warehouse duties would be to enter into the computer invoice-type information on every item that was delivered from the warehouse to any of the forty-eight schools in the Bibb County system. But it was several weeks before the computers to do this arrived. Then we had to wait for the man who had written the software program to come to the warehouse and instruct us in it.

Finally all the equipment arrived, we had finished being instructed, and I started entering data. The stock number and other information on every item that left the warehouse was supposed to be entered into the computer that same day, before I could go home. Some days it would be just impossible for me to do all of them, because at times there were more than 500 invoices in one day! On those worst days a lady from another office would come and help me in the late afternoon.

I worked frantically, trying to type faster and faster. Barbara Clinton came out to see how she could speed me up. I was moved to a better location, she showed me how it was faster typing numbers on the number pad rather than on the top line, and she got me a stand to hold the invoices, with a foot treadle to move the marker down one line at a time. All this helped, and now I was able to complete all the work about four out of five days. I had been told my work would be considered satisfactory if I completed the daily invoices most of the time.

I worked faster and faster, but this was a great strain. All day I sat alone, in one position, typing as fast as I could, never stopping or moving, unless going to eat or to the bathroom. This was the hardest job I had ever had. By the end of the day I would be totally exhausted.

It was important for me to keep doing my best, but deep down I realized there was no way I could keep working at this same pace. The Lord must have been with me, because it would have been impossible for me to have done so much work without Him. It was decided by everybody that this job was just too much for me and it was better for me to stop. It was a mystery to me why I had been given a job requiring superfast typing, as all my employers had known I was a slow typist before I started. It was hard for me to leave all of the good friends I had made there, and I knew I would miss them, but the job stopped at the end of the year.

Shortly after the warehouse job ended, my cousin Deryl told me she was going to be the director of Community Development for the United Cerebral Palsy office in Macon, where I had done my human services internship my junior year in college. Deryl said she needed me to help her, as a volunteer.

I thought to myself, "What can I do to help?"

But I found out. I went there and soon I was doing just about everything. One thing I often did was to go with Deryl all over two counties, collecting money out of the canisters on counters. Back at the main office I would count the money. I also typed, put papers in order, filed, and did other types of office work, especially when Deryl was busy. Sometimes other people would drive me to collect the money.

After working at the UCP office for a few months, Volunteer Macon selected Deryl and me to be on a TV program named "Everyday Folks." One of the local TV stations features some volunteer agency or person at the end of its nightly newscast every Monday. In this spot, the camera showed Deryl talking, and me counting the money. I was proud of all the hard work I did at the center, and that I was shown on TV.

I got some of the youth I was working with at the church interested in the United Cerebral Palsy center. Sometimes they were voluntary drivers for me in this work. One year they raised money for the annual United Cerebral Palsy Telethon by standing outside a shopping center and asking for donations. The Riverside youth and I presented a check for more than $100 to this organization on television.

One of the main projects Deryl and I worked on was to try to get a computer donated to the center. Among other functions, we felt it could be used to help the children communicate better. I wrote a letter to the TV star Henry Winkler, who hosted the UCP Telethon then, asking him for any ideas he might have on helping us get a computer. He never answered my letter. However, someone locally did give a computer to the center later.

Working at the UCP center gave me a good feeling that I was really helping out. Seeing the children there made me thankful to God for how far I have come in my life, since I had gone to this same UCP center, but then located elsewhere, when I was a small child. The children at the UCP center are aged five and under, and have all types of handicaps, such as muscular dystrophy, and many types of birth defects, but most have cerebral palsy. It will be great if some of these youngsters can go on to college!

Several months after I had started working at the cerebral palsy center, my longtime friend, Dr. Barbara Clinton, who is a professor of Computer Science, called and stated she was opening a new multimedia computer laboratory at Georgia College in Milledgeville. She asked me to come and work for her in the computer lab there, and I agreed. Barbara had helped get funding for her new facility by going all over the country taking part in workshops. I was the manager of the multimedia lab every Wednesday, and learned a lot. Barbara took me back and forth to Milledgeville, about thirty-five miles away, every week. I enjoyed working there, but it was a funny feeling being on a college campus without being a student.

After several months my father and I felt I needed a full-time job. We thought of the U.S. Census, which occurs every ten years, and was then about to start with the 1990 census. We contacted the local office of Congressman J. Roy Rowland, to find more information about this. We were surprised to learn that our cousin Jill Wynens was head of the Census for the Middle Georgia area. We contacted Jill and she said she was then hiring, and would be happy to have me "on board," if I could pass a test.

I took the test and it was very hard. I was afraid I had flunked it, but the lady who gave it said I not only had passed, I had made a good grade. She said I had been approved to work there, but before I could start, the FBI would have to check me out and clear me! I thought working for the Census must really be serious business, for everyone there to have to be checked out by the FBI.

In a few weeks they started me in the computer department of the Census. I was made Keyer Number 12, and I had to start reading this red notebook, which contained all you needed to know about your job. On every batch of work I keyed, I had to check it out with the notebook, which had all the numbers of the batches that came in. Then, when I got back to my desk, I would write on a little slip "K 12" (for Keyer Number 12), the date, the time started and time finished, and attach this slip to my batch. There was also a night shift of computer keyers. They started about 5:00 p.m. and worked until midnight or later. It took me several weeks to get comfortable with all my work duties.

About two weeks after I started working there it was great to discover that a lady who lives on my same street worked there too. We made a deal so I could pay her and ride with her every day. This relieved my mother from having to make that trip twice a day, and this arrangement worked out to everyone's benefit.

The Census job was good, but by its nature was temporary. In about six months my job ended, as the U.S. Census was nearly completed, and only a few supervisors and key people stayed on. This census data entry work had been very enjoyable and interesting for me.

The head lady, Jill Wynens, wrote me a great letter of recommendation, which said, among other things, that "The quality of Mr. Mann's work was the highest in the department."

After several months of searching, I found a new job, a very good one, at the Charter Northside Hospital, entering data into the computer for a doctor group that had offices in the hospital. I worked from nine to five on Mondays through Fridays. The offices were plush, and the people were wonderful.

One great thing about this place was that my good friend Tracy Jones was one of the head nurses there. I got to see her almost every day and we often ate lunch together in the hospital cafeteria.

I liked this job better than any I had ever had before. But this good situation did not last very long. After about six months of happy work I was looking forward to continuing there at least several more months, working with a new software program ordered by the main doctor in the group. The software came, but was not satisfactory, so all of a sudden there was nothing else for me to do, and I was let go.

For a couple of months afterwards I enjoyed not having to get up early and go to work. Also I was expecting the hospital to call me back soon to do some other new temporary job, as we both wanted, and which seemed likely. But this never happened.

However, I was not overly worried about getting a new job, as it had never taken me more than about six months before to find one. I applied for and received unemployment compensation for several months. I continued to work as a youth counselor at the church, and had more time to pursue this.

At first, after the hospital job ended, I did not work very hard at finding another, thinking Charter would call me back. But by March I realized I would have to start serious job hunting. So my father and I began making the rounds again. At least once a week we would spend the whole day, usually on a Wednesday, looking for places to work. As my father was now retired, he could devote more time to this.

We would try to go to fifteen or more places every week. We would always try to see the head person. On the days between, many hours were spent in making resumes, following up on leads, making phone calls, and preparing for the next week's job hunt. I found out that job hunting is just about a full-time job in itself!

At first it seemed that obtaining new employment would not be hard, as many people promised me work. But something would always seem to turn up at the last minute to prevent me from being hired.

I became discouraged, and learned the sad lesson that you cannot believe what a lot of people say. After several months of fruitless search, it seemed I was in line to become a media aide at any one of three schools in the public school system where there seemed to be openings. But none of these turned out.

That fall I did volunteer work for a political candidate, and he won. I thought that was a good omen. Shortly after that I got an irregular but paid job helping a businessman with his home computer business.

After several months of intense job hunting I finally obtained a temporary one with the City of Macon, doing computer work for the Fire Administration Headquarters. I found this to be a great place to work, and all the people were very good to me. My bosses seemed glad to have me, and I was certainly glad to be there, in a very nice office.

But I had only been hired as a summer intern, on a twelve-week job. This ninety-day period ended in September, but the good people there found some way to keep me on the payroll. Then, on December 20 my status was changed from temporary to permanent. I did not know this for sure until December 22, when the Fire Department people called my father and mother to meet with Chief Hinson (the head man), Chief Hartley, Chief Riggins, many of the ladies, some other firemen, and myself at a local restaurant for a luncheon to celebrate my new permanent status. My parents and I were overjoyed. About fifteen people were there, and I was the honoree and the center of attention. That was surely a great Christmas present!

The people at the Fire Department headquarters have been mighty good to me. Chief Hinson has taken me to lunch on occasions, to visit many of the fire stations, and to ride in a fire engine.

On weekends Chief Jim Hinson and I have been fishing, or I have driven the cart while he played golf! Chief Jim Hartley, the assistant head Chief, Chief Marvin Riggins, and the ladies there are also really good to me. This acceptance and comradeship means a lot.

A great thing about working in the central headquarters, and especially because the Fire Training Center is right next door, is that most of the city and county firefighters come through my office from time to time. In that way I have been able to meet most of this entire group!

It is a wonderful to belong to the brotherhood of the Macon/Bibb County Fire Department. The chiefs, the workers, and the firemen and firewomen are all fine people.

I have now been working at the Fire Department headquarters for more than a year. I enter information into the computer about the fire and emergency 911 calls, and the reports go to the state headquarters. This job has been good for me, and my fellow workers continue to treat me with respect. I sincerely hope and pray that I can keep this good position.

# *Summing Up*

I have always been happy natured, but with my cerebral palsy, growing up had many challenges for me. But aside from a few rough spots, my life has been good. Meeting many friends and teachers, I had fun along the way.

There have been many highlights in my life so far, but three stand out as probably the best.

The first was learning to walk unassisted. While unhandicapped children learn to walk by the time they are a year or so old, I was eight years old before I could walk alone, and then only with crutches and braces. But I have been able to walk—although very slowly—without any aids, since my late teenage years.

One of my greatest accomplishments was to be the first multihandicapped student to be fully mainstreamed by the Bibb County Board of Education in Macon, Georgia. I was not transferred to regular classes until I was in the eighth grade. I think every handicapped child, whether blind, deaf, mentally retarded, or with cerebral palsy or any other disability, has a right to be mainstreamed at an early age, if at all possible. No student should have to go through all I had to go through to get a full education in the public school system. My graduation from Lanier High School was fantastic.

The third and greatest highlight of my life, of course, was my graduation from Mercer University with a B.A. degree.

There is really no such thing as a nonhandicapped person. Everyone has some kind of handicap, whether it is big or small. Being blind or deaf is an obvious physical handicap, but a bad personality, meanness, lack of confidence, poor attitudes, even bad teeth, unusual body shapes, being dumb, or just being ugly, can be handicapping. Since no one is perfect, *everybody is special* in some way. Many people do not understand this, but they should.

❑

I hope this book shows that a handicapped person—like me—has all the hopes, fears, desires, and feelings of any "nonhandicapped" person. All of us, whatever our own particular handicap, want to be able to socialize, travel, love, read, learn, go to school, worship, and work at a useful job, just as everyone else, so far as our imperfections will permit. We all want to be given a full chance to lead a full life. I think that will happen when enough of us finally realize that, really, in the final analysis, everybody *is* special.

❑